DATE DUE

SEP 1 5 1995		SEP 1 5 1995	

Demco, Inc. 38-293

ANCIENT CRETE

ANCIENT CRETE

Photographs by
Leonard von Matt

Text by
Stylianos Alexiou
Nikolaos Platon
Hanni Guanella

FREDERICK A. PRAEGER, *Publishers*
New York · Washington

BOOKS THAT MATTER

Published in the United States of America in 1968
by Frederick A. Praeger, Inc., Publishers
111 Fourth Avenue, New York, N.Y. 10003

Copyright in Zurich, Switzerland, by NZN Buchverlag, Zurich, 1967
Translated from the German *Das Antike Kreta* by D. J. S. Thomson
English translation copyright in London, England,
by Thames and Hudson Ltd, London, 1968

Contents Map of Crete 6, 7

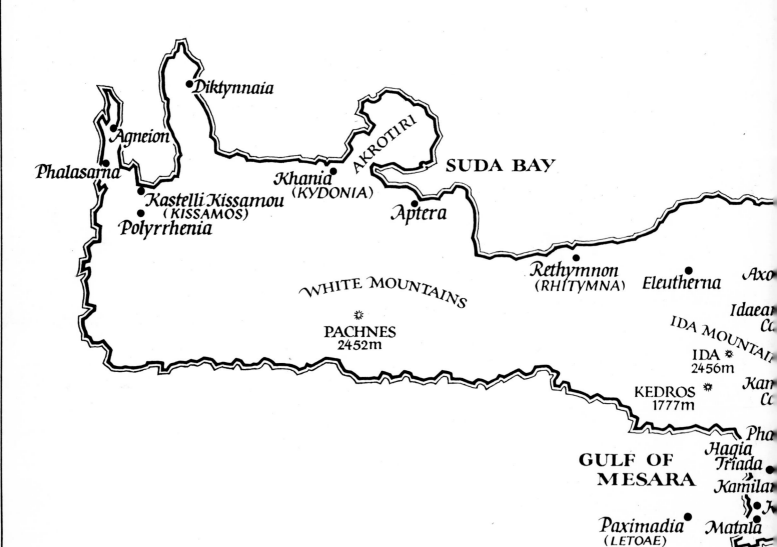

S E A   O F

Diktynnaia

Agneion

AKROTIRI

Phalasarna

Khania
(KYDONIA)

SUDA BAY

Kastelli Kissamou
(KISSAMOS)

Aptera

Polyrrhenia

Rethymnon
(RHITYMNA)

Eleutherna

Axo

WHITE MOUNTAINS

Idaea
Ca

IDA MOUNTAIN

✳
PACHNES
2452m

IDA ✳
2456m

Kam
Ca

KEDROS ✳
1777m

Ka

Pha

Hagia
Triada

GULF OF
MESARA

Kamilar

Paximadia
(LETOAE)

Matala

N

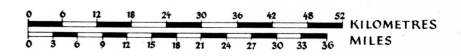

0   6   12   18   24   30   36   42   48   52
                                                                        KILOMETRES

0   3   6   9   12   15   18   21   24   27   30   33   36
                                                                        MILES

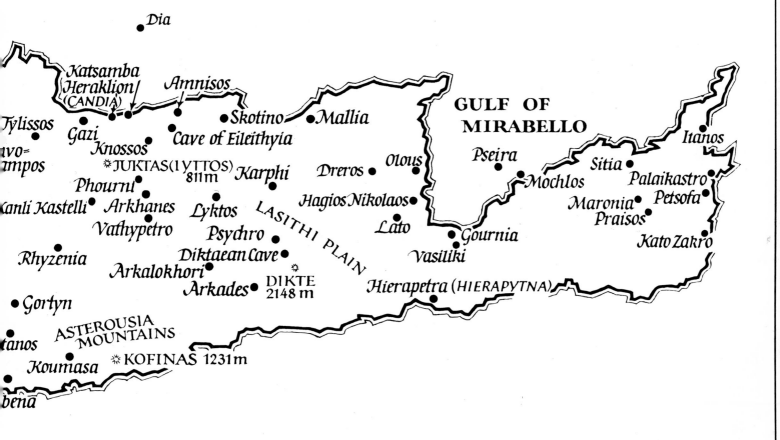

CRETE

Dia

Katsamba
Heraklion
(CANDIA)
Tylissos
Gazi
Knossos
Amnisos
Skotino
Mallia
Cave of Eileithyia
vo=
mpos
☀ JUKTAS (1YTTOS)
811m
Karphi
Dreros
Olous
GULF OF
MIRABELLO
Pseira
Itanos
Sitia
Mochlos
Palaikastro
Petsofa
Maronia
Praisos
Phourni
Kanli Kastelli
Arkhanes
Lyktos
Vathypetro
Psychro
Rhyzenia
Diktaean Cave
Arkalokhori
Arkades
DIKTE
2148 m
Gortyn
anos
ASTEROUSIA
MOUNTAINS
☀ KOFINAS 1231m
Koumasa
bena
Hagios Nikolaos
Lato
Vasiliki
Gournia
Kato Zakro
Hierapetra (HIERAPYTNA)

LASITHI PLAIN

LIBYAN SEA

STYLIANOS ALEXIOU

ART IN MINOAN CRETE

About the middle of the third millennium BC tribes from Asia
Minor migrated to the Cyclades, Crete and the Greek mainland.
They brought with them the use of copper and place-names
ending with the syllables -nthos, -sos, -tos, which are not found
in ancient Greek. It follows, therefore, that the people speaking
these foreign languages were also not Greek, although the
possibility cannot be excluded that they had some connection
with the Indo-European language group. Place-names ending
in -sos, for example, have been traced back to Luwian, an Indo-
European language of south-western Asia Minor. Ethnically the
Aegean immigrants belonged to the Mediterranean race, the
outstanding features of which are long heads (dolichocephalic),
brown eyes and black hair. At the same time a second wave of
colonists invaded southern Crete from Libya. With the introduction of copper and its increasing use for the manufacture of
tools and weapons, a new era dawned in Crete, which marked
the end of the primitive Neolithic way of life. There was a marked
growth in shipbuilding, which led to a flourishing trade between
the island and other parts of the eastern Mediterranean. The
active trade with Egypt and with the coastal population of Asia
Minor and Syria also had a positive influence on the arts. It was
from these countries that Crete acquired the technique of
working in stone and metal. By and large, however, the artistic
forms were developed along essentially Cretan lines.

At the beginning of the pre-Palace period, when the inhabitants of Crete were still living in primitive huts and the

8

settlements were little more than hamlets, the skill of the Minoan artist, his uninhibited spontaneity and his lively imagination emerged for the first time in pottery. Here we see the first flowering of what was to culminate in the Minoan Palace civilization.

The decoration on early pottery consists entirely of simple, vertical or sloping lines, which are either burnished (Pyrgos Style) or painted red (Hagios Onouphrious Style) or, very occasionally, painted white. These lines blend with the shape of the vessels. Subsequent modifications in form developed organically, almost of themselves, by a process of endless repetition, which by our standards was incredibly slow. So a very long time elapsed before the vases with curved bases – modelled on vessels made of leather – gave way to vases with flat bottoms. The potter's wheel, which was later to produce perfectly rounded forms, had not yet been invented, and the potter's hand was still free to play with the clay. This explains the world of fantasy which one finds in early Minoan pottery. Some vessels were fashioned into bulls, pigs, turtles and ducks, others into men or fruits, others again into boats or houses. In other cases, the form is so abstract that it is impossible to imagine what the potter had in mind. Even domestic pottery in daily use assumed peculiar shapes: cups, bowls and beakers were given strange, large handles or horn-shaped protruberances, which are striking departures from the basically austere form of the vessel.

The same inspiration becomes apparent later in the ivory seals. Birds, snakes, lions, bulls, monkeys, women with birds' heads and so on are reproduced in a very sculptural manner. The forms of the stone vessels are, by their very nature, more conservative. This is also true of the stone figurines of naked women, which are markedly austere in form, being based on foreign Cycladic models and therefore far removed from the traditional Neolithic forms of plump, steatopygous figurines. The small ivory figures are more native Cretan in character.

The tremendous creative urge of the potter is also apparent in most of the vases in the so-called Vasiliki Style. Their spouts are like the beaks of gigantic birds and the decoration is markedly different from that of the pottery which I have just described: the vessels, instead of being painted, have a fantastically mottled surface, which is produced while they are being fired. Just as the clay gave the potter freedom to experiment with all kinds of shapes, so the flames were left free to cover the 'tea-cup' or 'beaker' with large red and black spots.

At the end of the pre-Palace period, around 2000 BC, peace and prosperity reigned on the island. Crete was then thickly wooded with pine, cypress, oak and ilex and it was well supplied with rivers and springs. The Cretans were a happy, lively people, who lived in villages in the fertile plains or on the coast, from which small trading-fleets set sail for the Aegean islands and the coasts of Asia Minor and Egypt, returning with obsidian, gold, copper, silver and ivory. It may well be that the Minoan ships carried Cretan oil and Cretan wine in exchange.

Around 1900 BC the first large palaces were built by powerful rulers in the most fertile parts of the island, at Knossos, Phaistos and Mallia. The construction of such large buildings shows that the Minoan society was already highly organized and had considerable manpower – undoubtedly slave-labour – at its disposal. During the same period the hieroglyphic script gave way to the linear type of script. And for the first time the influence of Minoan culture became apparent outside Crete. Minoan pottery has been found in the island of Melos, at Lerna in the Peloponnese, and on the coasts of Syria and Egypt. Indeed, a Minoan colony was actually founded on Melos. Peace reigned on the island, the famous Pax Minoica. In all probability one king ruled over the whole of Crete. But for these favourable conditions Minoan art could hardly have blossomed, as it did, into a major culture.

Pride of place must go to pottery, the finest products of which are the so-called Kamares ware. Thanks to the potter's wheel, it was possible to produce finer shapes and vases with thin walls. But it is the incredible variety of decorative patterns, painted in bright and dark red, orange and white on the dark ground of the vessels, that is really impressive. These decorative designs – spirals, fringes, wheels, coils, hoops, hatchings and nets – are endless in their variety.

To begin with, the patterns are entirely abstract but gradually they become more and more representational. One of the most fascinating chapters in Minoan art is the transformation of abstract, linear and spiral motifs into branches, leaves, palms, and lilies, or into marine creatures such as octopus, cuttlefish, starfish and fishes or even into submarine reefs covered in seaweed. As the period of the Old Palaces drew to a close, the so-called naturalistic style began to emerge. The same trend can be observed in those vases on which flowers, dolphins, oysters and crabs appear in relief, frequently from casts made from the animals themselves. All this happened almost imperceptibly, without any break in tradition or continuity, without any sign of artificiality creeping in.

Human figures such as goddesses or dancing-girls are very rarely found on Kamares ware. Where they do occur, the human body is entirely subordinated to the vessel and becomes so much a part of the decoration that it is barely recognizable as a human figure.

This type of 'caricature' did not arise from any inability on the part of the artists to reproduce the human form in naturalistic terms but was quite deliberate, for there are seals and seal impressions from the same period which show a great variety of creatures more naturalistically portrayed. Animals, insects and humans are represented, while other designs are masterly repetitions of the abstract decoration of the pottery. In the period that immediately followed, the sequence is reversed; it is the carvings on the sealstones that influence the vase-painting. And the result of this exchange and cross-pollination within the arts, with each art-form remaining relatively autonomous, was the astonishing phenomenon which has become known as the Minoan culture.

The same synthesis of 'naturalism' and abstraction is apparent in the gold ornaments from the First Palace period, an outstanding example of which is the famous pendant with the hornets from Mallia. Two hornets on either side of a granulated disk, which represents the honeycomb, are shown depositing a drop of honey on it.

Stone vases also reveal – though to a lesser extent – this passion for surface decoration. The so-called 'bird's nest' form evolved into a flower (the so-called Blossom Bowl) with petals in relief.

As stylized as the human representations on the pottery are the clay figurines of the First Palace period, which were carried up to remote shrines on the mountain-tops. Their heads, which are as primitive or lacking in style as children's creations, resemble those of birds of prey. In many cases a cylinder is simply placed on the torso, on which only the most rudimentary features are outlined. The artists attached particular importance to the hair, which is presented in the most complicated, snail-like patterns.

Around 1700 BC the three palace complexes were destroyed in a great natural disaster, the cause of which must have been a powerful earth tremor or a rapid series of earthquakes. The chthonic snake-goddess whom the Minoans worshipped in another form as Britomartis or 'the sweet virgin', became the 'bringer of disaster' and destroyed her own children. Subsequently the palaces were rebuilt on a bigger and grander scale and the heyday of Minoan culture began.

During the Second Palace period (1700–1400 BC) abstract art was abandoned. Wonderful figurines in faience, bronze and terracotta, all on a small scale, even reveal attempts to reproduce physical details such as muscles and veins. But the precise rendering of anatomical details of the human body was not an end in itself; it served rather as a means of presenting a specific artistic type. Good examples of this are the sinuous, tightly-laced figures of votaries, bending their agile bodies backwards in a most convincing fashion. The artist is careful not to show the faces in detail. The imperceptible transition from one plane to another leaves one with the impression of youthful or even childlike features.

At this point one must pay special tribute to the insight and skill of the artist of this period, which enabled him to present his figures as moving freely in space, an achievement which is only equalled by Greek art some twelve hundred years later. The ivory acrobat from Knossos is shown in mid-air with arms stretched forward, without any visible means of support, in the act of leaping over the bull. The same boldness is apparent in the lithe attitudes, the back views, the foreshortened limbs, the quick, compact movements and the intertwining of men and animals on metal reliefs and on vessels of ivory and stone.

The artists continued to show a preference for relief vases which reach their climax in a series of remarkable ceremonial vessels, representing bulls, heads of bulls and lionesses or conch shells. On the other hand, the human figure does not appear on painted vases. The main reason for this is doubtless that the Minoans regarded an ivy-leaf or the tentacle of an octopus as more suited to the curved surface of a vase than the human body. Lovers of classical Greek art, which gives pride of place to the human figure, consider its absence from Minoan vase-painting as a defect. But are motifs from the plant and animal worlds not also artistic creations? Perhaps the real strength of Minoan art – what brings it closer to our own time – lies precisely in its awareness of nature. Unlike Greek art, which, as it developed, gradually lost its sense of space, Minoan art does not become absorbed in the mythology of human action.

The rapid and rhythmical evolution of Minoan art is nowhere so easy to detect as in the pottery of the Second Palace period. No sooner are forms assimilated than they are superseded by new ones, and the artistic expression changes from decade to decade without any break in the essential continuity of the culture. This is a phenomenon that only recurs in Greek art and, much later still, in the Italian Renaissance.

At the beginning of the period the shapes become more slender, while the decoration is less colourful than the Kamares Style. Before the white disappears altogether, it persists as a dotted line, while the orange survives as a band; the decorative motifs are confined to the extremities of the vases, while the main surface is filled with representations drawn either from the plant-world, as for example branches, leaves, lilies and other flowers, or from marine life, for example octopus, conch shells, cuttlefish, rocks and seaweed.

The human figure is one of the main themes in wall-painting but does not take the form of historical scenes or heroic figures from a mythical past, as is the case with Greek art. Such an approach was quite foreign to the Minoan artist. Divinities or mortals representing divine creatures, priests and votaries are depicted in their various roles, performing solemn religious rites, dancing or engaged in some ritual contest.

The paintings are often very small and freely executed. Series of pictures appear either as friezes above the gypsum facing on the walls of the rooms and chambers or as rectangular panels framed by painted fillets or rosettes.

Besides the human figure we find scenes from nature: brightly-coloured veins in the rocks, which become visible when the stone is cut or eroded by water, are employed for decorative purposes. Among the rocks grows the typical Cretan flora: wild roses, crocus, ivy, iris and lilies. Wild goats leap over crags and wild cats stalk fluttering birds. Everything is painted in simple, vivid colours.

In many paintings this landscape, so familiar to the Cretans, is the world in which the gods live and move. It can be seen as decoration pure and simple in the frieze of the partridges or in the frescoes from Amnisos with their red and white lilies. At the same time abstract motifs such as spirals, meanders and labyrinths also occur in the wall-paintings. Striking examples of the decorative art just mentioned are the paintings of dolphins and sea-urchins on the walls of the Palace of Knossos. For the decoration of ceilings an intricate pattern of running spirals is before long employed, which can be continued indefinitely.

Somewhat later, perhaps as a result of Egyptian influence, the human figures become larger. A particularly popular theme is religious ceremonial: on the walls of the narrow corridors of Knossos is an unending series of ritual processions, almost as if the artist was anxious to hold forever the constant movement of mortal creatures through these corridors. In accordance with tradition, the human face is always shown in profile, and the sexes are distinguished from one another by painting their bodies red and white respectively. The colourful impression conveyed by the paintings as a whole is enhanced by the treatment of the background, where white and black, and frequently red and yellow change into blue, representing the sky.

Constant movement is also a characteristic feature of the architecture. The large and the small palaces, the royal villas and the private houses are all built on several levels, and the façades, which are broken up by a series of projections, form a pattern of alternating light and dark walls. There are numerous large and small openings, courtyards, corridors, light-shafts, flights of steps, halls, colonnades, terraces, and rows of doors (polythyra) to break the monotony of walls and roofs and give the entire complex an air of great liveliness and variety. The wall-paintings in the halls, verandahs and forecourts serve to enhance the architectural interplay of light and shade.

The Minoan column – an inverted tree-trunk – conveys an impression of elasticity and tension which is in keeping with the general character of the building. A Minoan palace with Greek columns, the broad bases of which make them essentially earth-bound, would be inconceivable!

The Minoan artist's skill in 'composition' is seen to full advantage in the sealstones of the Second Palace period. The component parts do not appear juxtaposed, as they are, for instance, in the Mesopotamian cylinder seals, but in the round or elliptical shapes of this period are blended to form an organic whole. The composition is wholly adapted to the working surface, subject only to aesthetic demands and in no way dependent on the intrinsic nature of the subject-matter. In ritual scenes, for example, the figures of gods are no larger than those of men. As the artist had to fit them into a prescribed area, it is not always easy to recognize them as divine creatures. The highly sensitive touch of the Minoan artist is particularly apparent in the art of cutting sealstones, which calls for a degree of artistic sensitivity that can only be appreciated if one actually holds the object in one's hand.

After the appalling catastrophe of the volcanic eruption of Santorin around 1450 BC, the 'Palace Style' emerges at the end of the Second Palace period. This is characterized by the concept of a vase as a composite vessel in which base, body, neck and handle constitute separate entities, to be fashioned into a harmonious whole. This is a new approach by comparison with the old conception of a vessel as a coherent, plastic entity in itself. The same spirit is reflected in the decoration of the vessels: papyrus flowers – taken not from nature but from traditional Egyptian art – lilies, leaves, marine animals, rosettes, all these motifs are employed schematically and symmetrically over the surfaces of the vases.

The large amphorae and pithoi seem, for the first time, to take on monumental proportions and even the small vessels show a similar trend. Characteristic of this period is the artist's choice of decorative motifs, which would previously have been rejected as quite unsuitable, as for example birds, helmets, shields and, though less frequent, the human figure. The anti-naturalistic trend, the return to pure decoration, takes a form quite different from that of the earlier Kamares ware. The octopuses and the flowers lack the movement and the animation which they previously had and become once again mere abstractions. This also accounts for the absence of seaweed and rocks, which on the older vases conveyed an impression of space and introduced a note of realism.

The conscious striving for non-realism in the 'Palace Style' is also reflected in one final form which one might describe as an intermingling of forms. To take an example: birds are presented in such a way that it is impossible to recognize whether they are meant to be ducks or partridges. The same is true of the wall-paintings: the flora of a seascape in Knossos is not, as one might expect, demonstrably 'marine' in character. The dentated, unnatural tentacles of the argonauts move about in a fantastically unrealistic atmosphere.

Contrary to what some scholars believe, this artistic movement towards the abstract cannot be attributed solely to the growing influence of the Achaeans. In all probability the art of Crete, which was not subordinated to any religious cult, would have sought new modes of expression even if there had been no foreign influence and the period of ultra-naturalism would have produced a reactionary movement towards more abstract forms, these being the two poles between which art in any period oscillates.

Between 1400 and 1350 BC, for reasons that are still unknown, the palace complex of Knossos, the only one that existed at that time, was finally destroyed. Either fresh earthquakes were responsible or it may have happened during a revolt by the Achaeans of the mainland against their Minoan rulers, who, Evans assumes, had extended their rule to the Peloponnese and the Greek mainland. This theory is backed up by the assertion that the myth of Theseus, who killed the Minotaur, symbolizes the overthrow of the Minoan state by its former tributary subjects. When the inscribed tablets of Knossos were deciphered, however, the Linear B script was found to be early Greek. So the Achaeans had already occupied Knossos around 1450 BC and the cause of its final destruction after 1400 was not an Achaean invasion but more probably a war between the Achaeans of Knossos and the Achaeans of Greece. The third theory, that the disaster which led to the destruction of Knossos was a revolt by the Minoans against the Achaean conquerors would seem to be untenable, because the other Cretan cities had for the most part been reduced to ruins, abandoned or deprived of their power ever since the natural disaster of 1450 BC. Blegen and Palmer maintain, on the other hand, that the Palace of Knossos was finally destroyed not in 1400 BC but much later, around 1200 BC, together with the Mycenaean palaces of the Peloponnese.

At all events after 1400 BC the Achaeans were masters of the Aegean; the Mycenaean thalassocracy had taken over from the Minoans; Crete was overrun by Achaean settlers. The principal royal residence still seems to have been in Knossos but not on the site of the old palace-complex. New immigrants crowded into the island. Homer, who mentions the Achaean King Idomeneus as one of the participants in the Trojan War, speaks of the cities of Knossos, Phaistos, Gortyn, Lykastos, Milatos and Rhytion and of the Kydonians of west Crete.

What kind of art did this Mycenean period (1400–1100 BC), following the destruction of Knossos, produce? It is highly stylized, its decoration extremely formalized. The tentacles of the octopus, for example, of which there are usually four or six but sometimes as many as twelve, are disproportionately long, and the flowers have degenerated. In the so-called 'Close Style' the motif is entirely lost sight of in the plethora of hatching and incidental decoration. The same is true of the small sculptures, in which nature is presented in a deliberately stylized form. Parts of the human body such as the back, shoulders, torso, breasts, elbows or fingers and parts of the face such as the nose, eyes or eyebrows bear no apparent relation to the whole and are often enlarged out of all proportion. The neck becomes longer, the face more and more expressionless. By contrast with the figures in the Second Palace period, when the human body was seen as an organic whole, the postures are now rigid and unnatural. Clothing is reduced to a mere cylinder; the hands of the religious statuettes, which are now larger, are raised in the most stereotyped fashion. Art becomes more and more a formalized abstraction but without any of the potentiality or promise which was implicit in the abstract art of the pre-Palace and First Palace periods. The stylization of motifs in the closing years of the Mycenaean period marked the end of this particular type of art. And the same trend is apparent in the carving of the sealstones: birds, fish and flowers are grossly overstylized; only the essential parts of a chariot are shown; engraving is neglected and figures are depicted with disproportionately large, rigid limbs, which do not seem to be integral parts of the body; the art of adapting oneself to the material is lost, because artists are no longer able to work in hard stone. And the result, not unknown in our own day and age, is that, where the artist deliberately neglects technique, inevitably the reverse process sets in and technique deserts the artist.

The great culture, which had borne such astonishing fruits for one and a half thousand years, slowly fell into decay. Sometime after 1150 BC the tribes of north-western Greece began to move south again and conquer the Peloponnese. Before long the Dorians were in Crete and the ancient Minoan culture received its death-blow.

By contrast with Egyptian civilization, which is divided into dynasties established by written evidence, there is no such record of the history of the Minoan civilization. We must rely almost entirely on the results of archaeological research. Following his excavations at Knossos, Evans based his chronological breakdown largely on the evidence provided by the pottery. He maintained that there were three main periods, the Early, Middle and Late Minoan (generally known by the abbreviations E.M., M.M. and L.M.), and he subdivided each of these into at least three phases (I, II and III). Platon has suggested that a fuller and more precise terminology

and date-sequence can be achieved by basing the chronology on architectural development, a proposal which is adopted by Alexiou in his latest work, *Minoikos Politismos*, published in Heraklion in 1964. According to this interpretation, the *Neolithic* was followed by four main periods of Minoan civilization. The first, the so-called *pre-Palace period* (Proanaktorike periodos) lasted until about 2000 BC. Around 1900 BC palaces were built in various parts of central and eastern Crete (Knossos, Phaistos and Mallia); this is the so-called *First Palace period* (Palaioanaktorike periodos). These old palaces were destroyed by the first of several disasters, which probably took place around 1700 BC. Bigger and more beautiful palaces were built on the ruins. The golden age of the *Second Palace period* (Neoanaktorike perio-

dos) came to a sudden end in a second disaster around 1450 BC, which destroyed both the palaces and settlements near the coast and those in the interior. The view that the immediate cause of the disaster was a violent eruption of the volcano of Thera (Santorin) has been borne out recently by the excavation of a palace near Kato Zakro (east Crete). In the *post-Palace period* (Metanaktorike periodos), in which only Knossos took on a new lease of life, the Mycenaean population exercised an increasing influence on the Minoans. The infiltration by the Dorians in the *Subminoan period* marks the end of the Minoan civilization. As Minoan Crete conducted a lively trade with Egypt, the chronological table below gives the dynasties of the Old, Middle and New Kingdoms for purposes of comparison.

PLATON			EVANS		EGYPTIAN CHRONOLOGY	
Neolithic Period		6000–2600 BC	*Neolithic Period*		Predynastic (before 3100)	1–3 Dynasties (3100–2612)
Pre-Palace Period			*Early Minoan Period*		Old Kingdom	
	I	2600–2400		EMI		4–6 Dynasties (2612–2280)
	II	2400–2200		EMII		1st Intermediate Period
	III	2200–2000		EMIII		7–10 Dynasties (2280–2040)
			Middle Minoan Period	MMIa		
First Palace Period					Middle Kingdom	11–13 Dynasties (2133–1625)
	I	2000–1900		MMIb		
	II	1900–1800		MMIIa		
	III	1800–1700		MMIIb		
Second Palace Period					New Kingdom	2nd Intermediate Period (Hyksos)
	I	1700–1600		MMIIIa,b		14–17 Dynasties (1720–1527)
	II	1600–1500	*Late Minoan Period*	LMIa,b		18 Dynasty (1570–1320)
	III	1500–1400		LMII		
Post-Palace Period						
	I	1400–1320		LMIIIa		19 Dynasty (1320–1200)
	II	1320–1260		LMIIIb		20 Dynasty (1200–1085)
	III	1260–1150				
Sumbinoan Period		1150–1100	*Subminoan Period*			

THE PERIOD BEFORE THE GREAT PALACES

Neolithic Period 5000–2600 BC
Pre-Palace Period 2600–2000 BC

The first inhabitants of Crete were hunters and fishermen, but we do not know their origins. By about 5000 BC they had chosen places to settle in and had learned to till their fields and make their own pottery. The peasant population no longer lived in caves but in permanent dwellings which finally became grouped together in settlements.

It was not long before they began to bury their dead near the villages, in the large circular or domed tombs we associate with prehistory. They gave the deceased not merely objects of daily use but also ornaments and cult objects to take with them into the after-world. It is to these that subsequent generations owe at least part of their knowledge of the early inhabitants.

The religion of these early peoples was conditioned by their close links with the soil and the value they attached to everything that came out of it. They worshipped the Great Mother, a goddess of fertility. She was mistress of the animals but also goddess of the sea and ruled over the powers within the earth. The rich fertility of the island was the measure of her devotion to its inhabitants, in devastating earthquakes she showed her omnipotence. She was not worshipped in houses or temples but in caves or in the open air, where her devotees felt particularly close to her. Minoan religious imagery later found its way into Greek legend and Crete plays a not unimportant role in Greek classical mythology: Zeus himself, the Father of the Gods, was born and raised in a Cretan cave and he fathered the founders of the Minoan dynasty.

A glance at the map shows that during this pre-Palace period two areas on the island were particularly densely populated. In the Mesara Plain in the south, which at a fairly early stage became the granary of Crete, there is a marked abundance of tombs; in the eastern part of the island there were prosperous settlements, thanks to the intensive trade with the peoples of the East. And here, in specially selected places, are the sacred caves and shrines, in the folds of the hills, on steep, almost inaccessible slopes and on the tops of mountains.

Notes on the 18 illustrations that follow:

21
Bay of Matala with the small islands of Paximadia (Letoae) in the Gulf of Mesara. It was in such a bay, according to legend, that Zeus landed in the shape of a white bull bearing Europa, daughter of a Phoenician king, and mated with her. Their three sons Minos, Rhadamanthys and Sarpedon, were the future rulers of the island.

22
Entrance to the Diktaean Cave of Zeus on the Lasithi Plain in east Crete. According to the writers of classical antiquity, Rhea gave birth to Zeus in a cave in Crete. She had fled to the island under cover of darkness to save the child from the deadly clutches of her husband Kronos, who, afraid of being dethroned, devoured his own offspring. Not until 1886 was the cave on the slopes of Mount Dikte discovered by local inhabitants and subsequently identified as one of the island's early places of worship.

23
Votive offerings from the cave of the Diktaean Zeus on the Lasithi Plain in east Crete. In addition to vessels and objects from earlier periods, a large number of these small bronze bulls – the smallest

are only 5–7 cm. long – from the period around 1600 BC were found in niches and stalactitic fissures.

24

Sacred cave of Eileithyia at Amnisos on the north coast. Here the chthonic goddess of fertility was worshipped. Eileithyia was the Greek goddess of childbirth. At the entrance to the cave stands a fig tree. Excavations in 1929 led to the discovery of Neolithic relics and ritual markings on stalactites. Together with the near-by cave of Hagia Paraskevi at Skotino it ranks as one of the oldest shrines in the island.

25, 26

Cycladic idols from the round tomb at Koumasa (Mesara). In the tombs in the southern plain many such marble idols, imported from the Cyclades, were found: naked female figures with arms folded beneath their breasts. The head, in which the oval face is dominated by the bridge of the nose, is set on a high neck.

27

Entrance to the round tomb at Koumasa (Mesara). This type of circular tomb, consisting of slightly projecting layers of stone and usually with a dome-shaped roof, is particularly common in the main settlement area of early times, the Mesara Plain and the area surrounding it. Here, as in the Chrysolakkos burial-place at Mallia (p. 148) many dead were buried with their funerary offerings. The tombs served as a last resting-place for entire village communities. The diameter of the largest tomb at Platanos, including walls about 6 feet thick, is 60 feet.

28

Two-handled amphora; jug with handle, long spout and two eyes.

Both these Early Minoan vessels are decorated in red and brown on a light ground. The designs on the amphora are reminiscent of the pottery in the so-called Lebena Style, and the fine trellis pattern on the jug reminds one of the vessels in the Hagios Onouphrios Style (from the tomb of the same name at Phaistos and from the cave-tomb of Kyparisi at Kanli Kastelli in central Crete).

29

Round tomb at Hagia Triada at the western end of the Mesara Plain.

30

Landscape near Vasiliki in east Crete. On a low hill-top the complex foundations of a villa were excavated and vessels in the 'flame style' were found (see p. 31).

31

Beaked jug in Vasiliki style with 'flamed' decoration. The light-coloured, reddish surface of the jug has dark flame-patterns which were deliberately created while it was being fired. A special feature are the eyes inserted on both sides of the steep, dark spout.

32

Beaked cup of grey, veined limestone and small jug of polychrome stalactite, both from the island of Mochlos in east Crete. The Minoans learned the art of working stone from the Egyptians but the use of mottled stone for decorative purposes was specifically Minoan.

33

Early Minoan 'bird's nest' vases in various kinds of stone, the largest 8 cm., the smallest 4·5 cm. in diameter. The small bowls, which were placed beside the dead and undoubtedly had a religious sig-

nificance, have been found mostly in the Mesara region and in east Crete. In the right foreground a 'cruet', perhaps a forerunner of the religious 'kernoi'.

34

Lid of a green slate box from the island of Mochlos in east Crete. The handle in the form of a recumbent dog is a masterpiece of early miniature sculpture.

35

The island of Mochlos in the Gulf of Mirabello in east Crete, where some of the finest early Minoan stone vessels and precious gold ornaments were found. Mochlos was originally a peninsula but, following a natural disaster at some unspecified time, it became an island close to the shore.

36

Pyxis of slate with detachable cover from a cave-tomb at Maronia, in east Crete. Two rows of artistic spirals, which are also linked one with the other, surround the upper part of the box, while the lower part is covered with groups of parallel, incised lines (see cover in plate on p. 34). Upper and lower part are joined by twin bands with an oblique, indented pattern.

37

Ornaments of fine sheet gold from the island of Mochlos in east Crete. The gold leaves and flowers were found in the princes' tombs of Mochlos, gracing the bodies of the noble dead.

38

Rhyton, with handle at the back, in the form of a female bust in white painted terracotta from the island of Mochlos in east Crete. The position of the hands beneath the breasts is a divine gesture of fertility.

23

By the end of the third millenium BC the inhabitants of Crete had achieved a high standard of prosperity – not least through the steadily growing maritime trade with other islands and with the countries of the eastern Mediterranean. It is the beginning of that period of peaceful Minoan expansion to which the term 'pax Minoica' has aptly been applied. Merchants and craftsmen flourished, and the arts were constantly stimulated by the importation of new materials. Pottery became more refined, particularly with the invention of the potter's wheel. The funerary gifts and votive offerings in the caves, tombs and sanctuaries show a higher standard of craftsmanship and of artistry.

In addition to the growing settlements, centres with palace-like complexes appeared around 1950 BC at three points on the island: at Knossos in the rich vineyard country east of Mount Ida across the River Kairatos; at Phaistos on a hill overlooking the fertile Mesara Plain; at Mallia in the plain directly bordering on the sea. At these three centres one can see the transition from a peasant to an urban civilization. What their relations were with each other, whether two of them were subject to the largest of the palaces or whether each enjoyed complete autonomy is still not clear: the scripts which may perhaps one day throw some light on this – a hieroglyphic script and another more developed style of writing which scholars call Linear A script – have not yet been deciphered. But at least it is clear that the balance of power shifted towards the centre of the island and that this paved the way for the eventual supremacy of Knossos.

The old palaces survived for some three hundred years. About 1700 BC they were all reduced to ruins by some major disaster, the most likely cause of which was an earthquake. Apart from the remaining walls, column-bases and courtyards of these palaces, tangible evidence of this period is provided by enormous jars in which oil, grain and dried vegetables were stored and which were indicative of the wealth of the ruling class and the fertility of the island. They stood in cellars, which took up a substantial part of the total palace space, almost as if the amount of storage room had played a vital part in the planning of these Minoan residences.

The First Palace period reached its peak with the Kamares ware, which is a miracle not only of the art of pottery but also of painting. These brightly coloured vessels, which show such a wealth of imagination both in their shapes and in their decoration, are unique expressions of the spirit and artistic genius of a dynamic Mediterranean people.

Notes on the 14 illustrations that follow:

41
'Shepherd Bowl', from Palaikastro (east Crete). This deep bowl, without handles, was filled with little figures representing a shepherd and his flock of more than two hundred sheep. It is a unique example of a Middle Minoan votive offering.

42
Terracotta rhyton in the form of a bull from the round tomb of Koumasa (Mesara). Three tiny male figures are clinging to the head and horns of the animal. This clay libation-vessel provides a valuable clue to the origins of acrobatic bull-jumping which was later to become so popular.

39

43
Clay bird-jug from the round tomb of Koumasa (Mesara).

44
Terracotta figurine of a man with a dagger from the hill-top shrine of Petsofa (east Crete). In addition to the sacred caves, which served as places of burial or worship, hills and mountains were also regarded by the Minoans as places to meet divine presences. Believers flocked to these hill-shrines on pilgrimage, to offer their tokens of thanks or supplication in the open air. (Some impression of the exterior of such a 'hill-top shrine' can be gained from the relief rhyton recently discovered at Kato Zakro, p. 192). A great many votive offerings have been excavated: vases of all kinds, animals, human figures and even separate human limbs as offerings to a deity of healing. These figurines not only tell us a great deal about the nature of the deity these people worshipped – the arms folded beneath the breast, for example, are an ancient posture of worship – but also provide pointers to early Minoan fashions. The dress of the worshipper consisted of a loincloth with girdle and codpiece, a flat cap and soft shoes.

45
Woman's head with high coiffure from the hill-top shrine at Kofinas (south coast of central Crete).

46
Multi-handled sarcophagus in the form of a chest (larnax) from a tomb at Vorou (Mesara). Loops and button-shaped knobs were provided to tie the lid down with cord, which was sealed with a special seal (see the sarcophagus on p. 99 from the tholos tomb on the Phourni hill at Arkhanes, central Crete, with traces of the original sealing).

47
Multi-handled storage jar (pithos) with lid from Choumeri, eastern Mesara. In 1910 a peasant, ploughing his field, dug up this pithos quite undamaged and – like his Minoan forefathers – used it to store grain. The decoration between the looped projections and round the middle of the jar suggests the ropes which were needed to move these jars, which are often taller than a man.

48, 49
View from the palace hill at Phaistos towards the Ida range of mountains. The snow-capped mountain on the left is Mount Ida itself (8092 ft), the highest in the range; to the right of it are twin peaks known as the Digenis Saddle, under which the Kamares Cave lies (cf. note 51). On a clear day it is visible from the plain with the naked eye, for the entrance to the cave, 5500 ft above sea-level, is more than 100 ft wide and 60 ft high. In the centre of the picture are orange-groves bordered by olive trees.

50
Three Barbotine jugs. 'Barbotine' was the technique employed to produce a relief-like pattern on clay vessels by dabbing or pricking the surface. The eyes and beak-shaped spouts give the jugs a bird-like appearance. The jug in the centre dates from the beginning of the Kamares period (the style is a mixture of Barbotine work and Kamares painting).

51
Beaked jug in the Kamares Style with applied eyes. Between four white S-spirals runs a horizontal, oval motif embodying a red design. Kamares pottery, in which the white, red and orange colours stand out brilliantly against the metallic sheen of the dark background, took its name from the sacred cave on Mount Ida above the village of Kamares (see p. 48). In the cave, which was discovered in 1895, a large quantity of polychrome pottery was found.

52
Detail of a three-handled pithos in the Kamares Style. The vessel is encircled by three rows of white spirals and red leaves on a dark ground.

53
Above: beaker in the Kamares Style. The artist has captured to a remarkable degree the movement of a flower blown by the wind.

Below: small Kamares cup (left). White and red dots lend colour to the decorative pattern, which is reminiscent of the Minoan figure-of-eight shield. Kamares cup with dark rosettes (right). As the extremely thin wall of the cup is as delicate as an eggshell, this type of pottery became known as 'eggshell ware'. Here we see how the palace potters tried to reproduce gold and bronze objects in clay.

54
Two-handled storage jar decorated with palms. The decline of the Kamares Style is marked by the gradual introduction of plant life into the decoration. Naturalistic palm trees with patches of red grow out of an irregular ground.

43

I

About 1600 BC the new palaces were erected on the ruins of the old; bigger and more splendid than their predecessors but built to the same basic design: round a rectangular central court are grouped four blocks, each comprising countless small rooms and halls, courtyards and colonnades, staircases, corridors and storehouses. They are not arranged according to any clear, symmetrical plan but seem to have been added on quite arbitrarily. The spaciousness and complexity of these buildings account for the eventual change in the meaning of the word 'labyrinth', which the Greeks – as a Linear B text has confirmed – applied to the royal palace of Knossos but which was originally derived from 'labrys' or 'double axe' and meant simply 'House of the Double Axe'. The focal point of all the palaces is the central courtyard which runs north and south and has inner façades of several storeys, which enabled it to be used, together with the open, terraced spaces of the so-called 'Theatral Areas', for ceremonial functions and games. Common to all the palaces is a west wall, which is largely closed and which adjoins yet another open courtyard. All the palaces have 'Sacred Precincts', which are columned rooms with prayer-niches and lustral baths, three-naved sanctuaries, and treasure repositories in which objects dedicated to the deity were stored. Finally on the ground floor of every west wing there are extensive storage-rooms or 'Magazines'.

The Palace of Knossos is the most important of the palaces built in the golden age of Minoan civilization. In the depression between the Ida and Dikte mountains, where the road from the Mesara approaches the northern coast of Crete, the massive ruins of a very early settlement were found, forming the lowest level. After the destruction of the old palace, a princely family built a new palace-complex, which covered two and a half acres and in its heyday is said to have contained more than 1300 rooms in four and five storeys! It spreads over the Kephala Ridge, its east wing dropping down in stages to the River Kairatos, its south wing to the Vlychia Gorge. It lies only four miles from the sea, and formed part of a Minoan town among beautiful vineyards, which stretch up the valley towards Mount Juktas, silhouetted against the southern sky.

Crete was a fertile island, which at that time was also thickly wooded with cypress, pine and oak. The mountains provided ample water to keep the rivers running even in summer. From the beginning of the second millennium Crete became increasingly prosperous, building up a large merchant fleet and establishing bases on the Cycladic islands. The Cretans carried on an active trade with places on the nearer and the more remote coasts of the Aegean and the Mediterranean and even exercised a certain control over the maritime traffic. Since Crete now became the leading maritime power in the Aegean, historians have come to refer to this as the age of Minoan 'thalassocracy'. This explains why the palaces had no need of fortifications: as there was no enemy, the Cretans did not feel called upon to protect themselves against aggression.

The Cretans' state of contentment finds expression in the graceful spontaneity of Minoan art which prefers the small and the delicate to the monumental and heroic.

Large works of sculpture were unknown in Minoan Crete; reproductions of the human figure were hardly more than toy-like in size. The finest achievements of Minoan art were in the field of seal-engraving: in the tiny space of a sealstone minute figures and even entire scenes were engraved, which can only be 'read' with the help of a magnifying-glass. And the same is true of painting, which is frequently on a miniature scale. Pictorial art was always subordinated to architecture and served to enhance the general layout and decor of a room. With the exception of the giant pithoi, the storage vessels in the palace magazines, the objects with which the Minoan surrounded himself were on the small side and indeed he himself was small and compactly built.

There is yet another factor which is worth noting: Minoan art grew out of the mutual relationship between man and nature, out of man's submission to the magic appeal of nature. Flowers and animals decorate their beautiful pottery and feature in gaily coloured scenes, while lightly-clad, gliding female figures and slim-hipped youths grace the frescoes. There are no warlike scenes; the accent is on a people which congregates for ceremonial processions, for sporting contests and ritual games. So posterity is left with a picture of a talented, dynamic, nature-loving people, whose art still – after three thousand five hundred years – casts its spell over us.

II

The great palace-settlement of Knossos was excavated at the beginning of the present century. That it was discovered at all is as astonishing as the subsequent prolonged excavations themselves. For cen-turies the glorious civilization of the Minoans had existed only in Greek legend, in the myths of King Minos and the Minotaur, the man-bull and, with the help of Minos's labyrinth of the palace; of Daedalus, architect of the palace, and his son Icarus; of Theseus, who killed the bull and, with the help of Minos's daughter, Ariadne, found a way out of the maze of rooms. Had these myths not been taken seriously, the Minoan civilization, the earliest great civilization in Europe, would not have been unearthed at this spot.

The first of those who came to be associated with this historic discovery was a Cretan merchant, Minos Kalokairinos, who was passionately interested in the island's archaeology and who in 1878, during the Turkish occupation, was digging in the hilly olive-groves near Knossos when he came upon ruined masonry which he recognized as part of a larger building. Squared stones bearing masons' marks and twelve large pithoi came to light – they were part of the western magazine of the Minoan palace. Of the more than three hundred objects found, Kalokair-inos presented some to the museums in Paris, London, Rome and Athens, as well as to the collection of the 'Society of the Friends of Culture' at Heraklion. (This 'Philekpaideu-tikos Sylogos Herakleiou' was sub-sequently responsible for founding the Archaeological Museum in this town). A newspaper report of these early finds caught the eye of Hein-rich Schliemann, the man who, thanks to his belief in the accuracy of Homer's reports, had discovered Troy and Mycenae. Equally convinced that he could prove the historical existence of the Palace of Minos and the Labyrinth, he went to Crete to negotiate with the Turks for the purchase of the supposed site. The negotiations fell through. It was not until after the Graeco-Turkish war and the end of Otto-man rule, that Crete achieved its autonomy and systematic archaeo-logical excavation became possible.

In March 1900 Arthur Evans began digging at Knossos. For more than 25 years the English archaeologist supervised the exca-vations with tireless energy and with the assistance of Duncan Mac-kenzie and a staff of experienced archaeologists, architects, artists and technicians. He devoted the whole of his large private fortune to this work and succeeded in bringing to light a Minoan civilization which until then had only existed in legend: the Palace of Minos. His monumental four-volume work, *The Palace of Minos*, 1921–1936, is an account of the development of the Minoan civilization and con-tains extremely valuable pictures and sketches of the archaeological treasures that were unearthed.

Evans's work culminated in his reconstruction of individual sec-tions of the palace, a remarkable feat of creative imagination which gives the modern visitor a graphic picture of Minoan architecture; he can visualise the rooms in which the rare vessels stood and were used and he can feel the atmosphere of ceremonial solemnity in the Throne Room. It is true, of course, that the cedarwood columns, which were destroyed by fire in the final catas-trophe, have been replaced with concrete replicas, that the rooms now have concrete ceilings and that the ceilings are supported by iron girders. In those parts of the build-ing which have been painted, the colours jar, and one is shocked by the style of the painted copies in the corridors and halls. Today the work of reconstruction is carried out with more discretion and attention

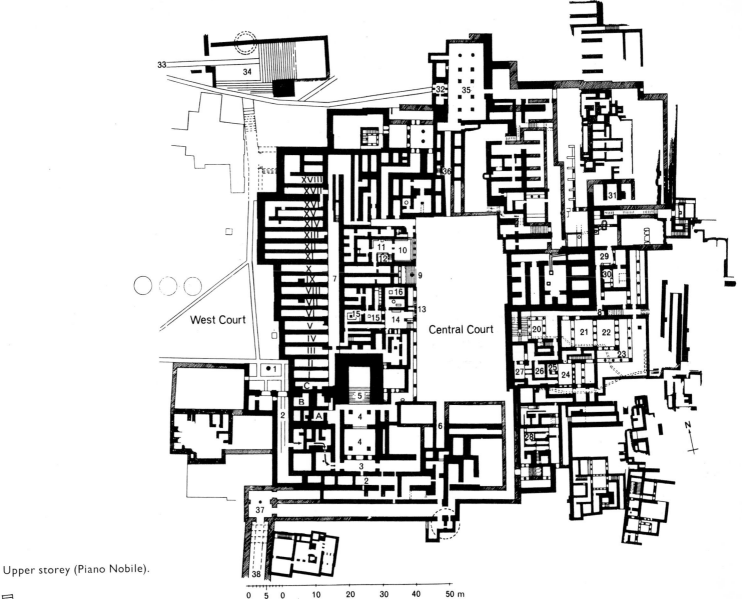

West Court

Central Court

Upper storey (Piano Nobile).

The Palace of Knossos

1 West Propylon
2 'Corridor of Processions'
3 Light well
4 South Propylaea
5 Staircase to Piano Nobile
6 Corridor of the 'Prince of Lilies'
7 Corridor of West Magazines
8 Corridor of East Block
9 Staircase to Piano Nobile
10 Ante-room
11 Throne Room
12 Lustral bath
13 Tripartite sanctuary
14 Ante-room
15 Pillared crypts
16 Treasure repositories
17 Santuary with 3 columns and 3 pillars
18 Hall with 2 columns
19 Hall with 6 pillars
20 Grand staircase

21 'Hall of the Double Axes'
22 King's Megaron
23 Colonnade
24 Queen's apartments
25 Bathroom
26 Treasure repository
27 Toilet room and W.C.
28 'Shrine of the Double Axes'
29 Potters' workshop
30 Lapidaries' workshop
31 Magazine of the giant pithoi
32 North entrance
33 'Royal Road'
34 Theatral Area
35 Hall of Pillars
36 Raised causeway
37 South-west entrance
38 Stepped portico

A, B, C and I–XVIII West Magazines.

57

to detail. And yet Evans's reconstruction was based entirely upon actual finds, upon fragments of pottery, sealstones and frescoes. Whatever one may think of the scientific, to say nothing of the aesthetic value of his reconstruction work, one must not forget that Evans's over-all picture of the Palace of Minos and of a civilization that spanned more than a thousand years is still valid today. Fresh excavations continue to bear this out long after his death. Just how illuminating his work is as a guide only becomes clear when one makes a tour of the palace ruins.

III

The main entrances to the New Palace were situated to the north, west and south. Today one enters the palace from the west. A paved path runs across the West Court to the western façade of the palace, of which part of the base about 3 feet high (the so-called 'orthostat base') is still standing. The palace wall must be visualized without windows on the ground floor (cf. note for plate on p. 78). On the south side of the forecourt one passes through a propylon (1) into a long passage (2), which is known as the 'Corridor of the Processions', because two long rows of men bringing offerings were depicted on each wall. The 'Cup-bearer' in the Archaeological Museum is one of some five hundred life-size figures from this frieze. After 25 yards the corridor takes a right-angle bend to the east and reaches a light well (3), where three doors originally led into two pillared porticoes (4). Beyond these propylaea is a broad staircase (5) which leads up to the Piano Nobile.

At its eastern end the 'Corridor of the Processions' turns northwards and leads (6) to the southern end of the Central Court; this runs north and south and covers an area of 55 by 30 yards. On its long sides lie the two main blocks, each divided by a corridor; the one in the west block (7) runs north and south parallel to the Central Court, while the one in the east block (8) runs from west to east and at right angles to it. In consequence there are four 'quarters' which make inspection of the excavation site somewhat easier.

The palace-complex which is grouped round the Central Court was of special significance, as its rooms were used for religious ceremonies. A sketch by Evans shows the inner façade as having two storeys and splendid proportions. To the right of a grand staircase (9) which leads up to the Piano Nobile is the entrance to the Throne Room. On the outer wall of the anteroom (10) is the rounded corner, which dates back to the Old Palace and was treated with great reverence. A short flight of steps leads down to the antechamber, in the middle of which stands an enormous red stone basin (p. 67). Although it was found in a northern corridor, which links the Central Court to the West Magazines, Evans placed it here because he believed it had served as a kind of aspersorium in the Throne Room. A double door with pillar leads to the Throne Room (11) itself. The tall gypsum throne, the low gypsum wall-benches and the fresco of monumental griffins all serve to underline the royal character of this room. Opposite the throne, steps lead down to a subterranean room (12), a 'lustral bath', which was not in fact a bath, as there is no drain, but had some ritual significance concerned with purification and prayer. Underground rooms of this kind were also found in the old palaces. Whether sacred snakes were kept in them is not known. Memories of early Minoan cave sanctuaries may have played a part in their construction.

When the Throne Room was excavated, the floor between the throne and the central doors was littered with those flat, onion-shaped alabaster vases which are known to have been used for storing oil in the rooms. They were strewn around a large, overturned pithos, as if the smaller vessels were being filled with oil when disaster suddenly struck. The palace and those who had gathered there for a religious ceremony were overwhelmed. Through this unusual find, the Throne Room has left an eye-witness account of the destruction of the palace.

To the left of the staircase leading to the Piano Nobile lies the complex of rooms which served some sacred purpose, the tripartite sanctuary (13) with two pairs of columns at the front of the aisles and a taller column at the front of the nave, the pillar crypts (15) with their anteroom (14) and the Treasure repositories (16), from whose underground vaults a large number of precious ritual objects were unearthed, as for example the Snake Goddesses and their attributes (pp. 68, 69, 71–73).

On the western side of the west corridor (7) lies the long row of magazines of varying lengths and widths, eighteen of them filled with pithoi, some of which are still standing where they were found.

On the upper floor of the West Block, which, as already mentioned, is reached by staircases from the south (5) and from the middle of the Central Court (9), the distribution of the rooms can only be surmised. They were occupied by persons of rank. Evans identified a hall with central columns, a vestibule and the sanctuary with three columns and three pillars (17) on the east side of the corridor; on the west side, in other words over the northern parts of the ground-floor magazine, an almost square hall with two columns (18) and to the north of it a second, rectangular hall with six pillars (19), in which the remains of a double fresco of sitting and standing people were found. From the shape of the seats, it is known as the 'Camp-stool Fresco'. The woman's head reproduced on p. 80 may form a part of it. Originally the staircase from the Central Court led up to a third storey.

To the south of the multi-storeyed corridor running east and west (8) the private apartments of the royal family were excavated. In the Old Palace the living-quarters – probably for climatic reasons – had been moved to the slope running down to the river and the various storeys had been connected by a grand staircase (20). Evans was able to excavate this almost undamaged (p. 65), except that the wooden columns, which were destroyed by fire, had to be replaced by stone ones. One descends comfortably down the broad, shallow steps from the Central Court to the royal apartments. A shaft beside the staircase incorporating pillars on three sides provided the lower parts of the building with light and air. These light wells, which rise several storeys and are open to the sky, can be found in various parts of the palace.

A corridor with beautiful, original paving leads to the 'Hall of the Double Axes' (21), so called from the double axes carved in the wall of an adjoining light well, and to the King's Megaron (22), a room with doors on three sides. In the fourth wall Evans found the remains of a wooden throne with a canopy. Connected by folding doors, the two rooms could be converted into one and used as an audience-chamber. In front of the Megaron was a covered colonnade (23) which provided shade and coolness.

The Queen's apartments near by (24) were decorated with particularly beautiful frescoes – the best known are the dolphins in the water and the dancing-girl with flowing hair (p. 81). In the Queen's bathroom (25) stood a painted clay tub and in a room at the back (27) there was even a lavatory with a water-flushing system.

Through the entire palace the water-supply was admirably organized. As early as the beginning of the second millennium BC spring-water was brought in from outside through skilfully-made clay pipes. A gigantic, white limestone well 50 feet deep and 25 feet in diameter was sunk at the south-eastern end of the palace down to the level of the river-bed; unfortunately this impressive structure collapsed shortly after it was excavated. It has been compared with the Pozzo di San Patrizio at Orvieto, as it too was found to have a winding passage hewn out of the walls and spiralling downwards the whole depth of the well. But the Italian well only dates back to the sixteenth century AD! The Minoans had also mastered the art of conducting water under pressure and, as one picture in the 'House of Frescoes' on the 'Royal Road' shows, they opened up springs in the palace gardens.

To the north of the corridor running east and west (8) lay the workshops of the potters (29), the lapidaries and stonemasons (30), the goldsmiths and other craftsmen.

There were also storerooms here. The biggest of the pithoi found in the palace stood in the east wing (31). The sight of these 'giants' makes the story of Glaucus, son of Minos, that has come down to us entirely credible; legend has it that, while the boy was catching a mouse or while playing, he fell into a pithos of honey and was suffocated.

Anyone approaching the palace from the residential quarters of the Minoan town to the west and north or from the ports of Katsamba and Amnisos arrived at the north entrance (32). The approach was made by way of the 'Royal Road' (33), which was about 13 feet wide, consisted of a slightly raised, paved causeway with a cobbled strip on either side, and led up to an open stairway (pp. 63 and 64). Turning to the left, the visitor found himself in the 'Theatral Area' (34), while to the right stood the gateway to the north-west corner. One then passed through an antechamber into a pillared hall (35) (Evans called it the 'Customs House'), at the south-west corner of which one reached the foot of a causeway (36), which vehicles could also use. This gently-rising approach to the central courtyard had been considerably wider in the Old Palace but when the palace was rebuilt it was made narrower and enclosed within walls, over which rows of columns were erected. The relief frescoes on the walls showed scenes with bulls (p. 74).

The rooms in the south wing descend towards the Vlychia Gorge. At the south-west end of the palace a stepped portico (38) had been cut out of the hillside, leading down to the river. A viaduct with arches 26 feet high and 10 feet wide, which dated back to the First Palace period, stretched across to the other bank, where stood a building which may have served as a guest-house. Evans called it 'the Caravanserai'. Visitors to Knossos from the warmer southern climate of the Libyan Sea or from the Mesara could refresh themselves and their animals at the fountains and baths.

The remaining subsidiary buildings do not call for detailed comment. At what used to be the end of the 'Royal Road' lay the Little Palace, second largest of the buildings excavated at Knossos. It was discovered when the search for the western end of the 'Royal Road' was being made. It was built in the closing stage of the Second Palace period and was used primarily for ritual purposes. Valuable ritual objects such as the libation vessel in the form of a bull's head (p. 70) were found in pillared crypts.

The so-called 'Royal Villa' in the north-eastern part of the palace, a two-storey house built out into the Kairatos valley, and the 'Great Temple Tomb' on the Minoan road to Arkhanes and the Mesara, both belong to the close of the Second Palace period. The two-storey Temple Tomb, which was the last resting-place of Minoan princes and consisted of an entrance hall, a pillared vault and an underground burial-chamber, was used not merely to house but also to worship the dead.

THE NEW PALACE OF KNOSSOS

Notes on the 30 illustrations that follow:

63
The 'Royal Road' on the northern fringe of the palace. The slightly raised, paved causeway forks before the cypresses, then leads to the open stairway of the so-called theatre.

Originally it linked the Little Palace in the west with the north entrance to the main palace.

64
Open stairway in the so-called 'Theatral Area' at the north entrance to the palace, as seen from the 'Royal Road'. The shallow steps forming the two flanking terraces could accommodate approximately 500 spectators, who watched the religious ceremonies or sporting contests, standing. Between the two terraces, which are at right angles to each other, there is a high platform, which Evans called the 'Royal Box'.

65
Main staircase in the east wing of the palace (Evans's reconstruction). The staircase is flanked by a light well. Between the columns – the diameter of Minoan columns increases from the ground up, culminating in a torus capital – frescoes are visible, which show Minoan figure-of-eight shields hanging in front of a frieze of interwoven double spirals. The door on the right leads into the 'Hall of the Double Axes'.

66
The Throne Room of the New Palace. The throne with the seat hollowed for comfort and the high back with its scalloped edge stands in its original place. It is carved from a single block of gypsum but, as can be seen from the legs, it was modelled on wooden thrones. On the wall above the low gypsum benches is a colourful frieze showing huge griffins lying amongst papyrus-stems.

67
Ritual bowl of red stone in the antechamber of the Throne Room.

68
The small 'Snake Goddess'. Detail of statuette shown on p. 69.

69
The small 'Snake Goddess'. Faience statuette from the underground treasure repositories of the central sanctuary: height 29·5 cm. The Minoans worshipped the Great Mother Goddess, a goddess of fertility, who gave birth every year to a god who, like the vegetation, died at the end of the year to be reborn in the following spring. As earth goddess she appears in many forms, very frequently as 'Mistress of Animals' (see p. 171, lower picture), here as the Snake Goddess. In each hand she holds a small, writhing snake, which always accompanied the earth goddess and which the Minoans held sacred. In the palaces special rooms were set apart for the breeding and care of snakes and they contained special snake-vessels. The goddess's dress illustrates Minoan women's fashions: an apron is worn over a bell-shaped skirt with horizontal flounces; the upper part of the body is clad in a bodice, which leaves the breasts exposed. On either side of the dress, which covers the feet, lie mussel-shells of faience, which were found in the same treasure-chest with other devotional objects (e.g. those on pp. 72 and 73). On the goddess's cap-like headgear sits a sacred animal (a small beast of prey or a cat).

70
Libation-vessel in the form of a bull's head in black steatite. This precious rhyton was designed to contain holy liquids. The neck has an opening for pouring in the liquid, which runs out again through the upper lip. The eyes are of rock crystal and jasper, the horns

of gilded wood. The finely modelled forelocks and the delicate carving on the head reveal the high artistic standard of the palace workshop. The bull played a major part in the Minoan religion. Recent excavations in eastern Asia Minor have established beyond doubt that bull-worship came to Crete from the East, where it is known to have been practised in the sixth and fifth millennia BC. The entire bull, the bull's head and even the bull's horns (the so-called horns of consecration) were sacred symbols (see pp. 90, 121, 192). To overcome the animal in any way, whether by sacrifice or by leaping over it (p. 76), was to appease the deity.

71

The large 'Snake-Goddess' (detail). Faience statuette from the underground treasure repositories of the central shrine, height 34·2 cm. Snakes are coiled round the goddess's arms, shoulders and hips, forming a knot in front of her body. In her right hand, which hangs down at an angle, is a snake's head, while a second appears over the turban-like headdress. The goddess is clad in an unflounced skirt and open-breasted bodice over a tight corset.

72, 73

Faience reliefs of a wild goat or antelope, which is suckling its two young, and a cow with its calf. The small reliefs, which are opposed and undoubtedly belonged together – perhaps inlaid in wood – were found, together with the snake-goddesses (pp. 69 and 71) and other devotional objects, in the underground treasure repositories of the central shrine in the west wing of the palace. They too are symbolic representations of the great Goddess of Fertility.

74

Part of the coloured relief of a bull. From the north entrance to the palace a drive led up to the central courtyard. There were walls on either side surmounted by columned passages. The bull's head was part of a major composition on the walls, which depicted the capture of a bull in an olive-grove. This fragment, 44 cm. high, is one of the most impressive works of art of the sixteenth century BC.

75

Antechamber of the Pillar Crypts with gypsum bench. The two crypts behind, which were supported by columns, are among the holiest sanctuaries set aside for religious ceremonies. Two pillars, on which double axes are incised, have special grooves at the base for libations. The presence of pillars indicates that the room in question was held particularly sacred. The memory of earlier cave-shrines may have played a part in this association.

76

Bull-leaping. Fresco from a frieze in a small courtyard in the east wing. One of the most important ritual spectacles for the Minoans was bull-leaping, a highly dangerous feat practised by young men and women alike. The acrobat stood motionless while the bull charged him, then seized the animal's horns and, as the bull reared its head, allowed himself to be flung into the air. With one leap over the bull's body the acrobat landed on his feet behind the animal. This fresco shows the three main stages of the jump.

77

Bull-leaper in ivory. The acrobat, who is shown in the air, was one of a group of figures depicting the bull-sports. The flowing hair was made of gilded bronze wires. In the undamaged hand the tension of the muscles and veins is clearly reproduced.

78

'Town Mosaic'. Miniatures in faience representing Minoan houses. These pieces, though only 3–5 cm. high, give one some idea of the domestic architecture of the Minoan private house: ashlar walls held together by thin layers of clay, half-timbered, with doors and framed windows. There are no ground-floor windows, and in this they resemble the exterior of the palaces. The centre plaque on the extreme right is the only one that does not seem to represent a house. Its edges are bent inwards, reminding one of a 'portable' stone altar (see p. 98, right).

79

'The Blue Bird', a garden fresco from the 'House of the Frescoes' on the 'Royal Road' north of the palace.

80

Woman's head, known as 'The Parisienne'. This fragment may belong to the so-called 'Camp-stool Fresco' from the sanctuary with six pillars in the upper storey of the West Block. The knot which is so artistically attached to the neck was identified by Evans as a 'sacral knot', a sacred symbol which also sometimes appears in faience.

81

Fragment of a fresco of a dancing girl with flowing hair from the Queen's Megaron.

82

Alabastron with octopus. The body and tentacles of an octopus are coiled artistically round the vase. Minoan artists have shown convincingly on much of their pottery that the octopus can be beautiful.

83

Gaming-board in ivory with inlay of lapis lazuli, rock crystal, silver and gold; the pieces used in the game, which are about 8 cm. high, are also of ivory. Opinions differ about whether this board, measuring 105 × 58 cm., was in fact used for some game or for fortune-telling.

84

Above: Three ivory seals representing animals. The lioness's head, the recumbent lion and the two monkeys at play all have holes through which a thread could be inserted in order to fasten the seal, perhaps to the wrist. In the Cup-bearer fresco, one of a long series of bearers of gifts in the 'Corridor of the Processions' of the West Block, the man is wearing such a seal attached to his wrist.

Below: A mould (right) for a gold earring. A particularly charming feature is the decoration of the small loop with a mulberry. One realizes what Homer meant when in the Iliad XIV, 183 he describes earrings as 'mulberry-like pendants' (moroenta ermata). The left-hand illustration shows a plaster impression taken from the mould.

85

Seven seals made from different stones. From top to bottom: brown agate with two horses; chalcedony with two beakers; red jasper with two birds; agate; green jasper with wild goat (three chased surfaces); rock crystal with two fish; sardonyx with lion.

86

Gold seal-ring from the royal tomb at Isopata near Knossos, depicting a ritual dance. Three female figures are dancing round a fourth in a flowery meadow. All are wearing Minoan costumes and have their arms raised in prayer or supplication. In the background a small (female) figure appears poised in the air.

87

Gold earring in the form of a bull's head (bucranium) from the cemetery of Mavro Spelio near Knossos. Delicate gold grains are soldered on to the entire surface of the skull (granulation technique). This highly stylized form is reminiscent of a bunch of grapes or mulberries (cf. p. 84, lower picture).

88

Three-handled amphorae with papyrus motif in the 'Palace Style' dating from the last Palace period. The 'Palace Style' replaced the 'Floral' and 'Marine' styles but was confined to Knossos.

89

Three-handled pithos of alabaster with spiral intaglio pattern on the upper rim and raised spiral pattern on the side.

90

Storage vessels (pithoi) at the foot of the staircase leading to the upper floor (Piano Nobile) of the West Block. The largest magazines in the palace were situated here in the West Block next to the South Propylaea. In 18 passages of varying lengths leading off a corridor, some 150 pithoi were found standing in rows – there would have been room for 400 of these storage vessels, representing a total capacity equivalent to 17,000 gallons. They were used to store the palace supplies of oil, wine, grain, vegetables and honey.

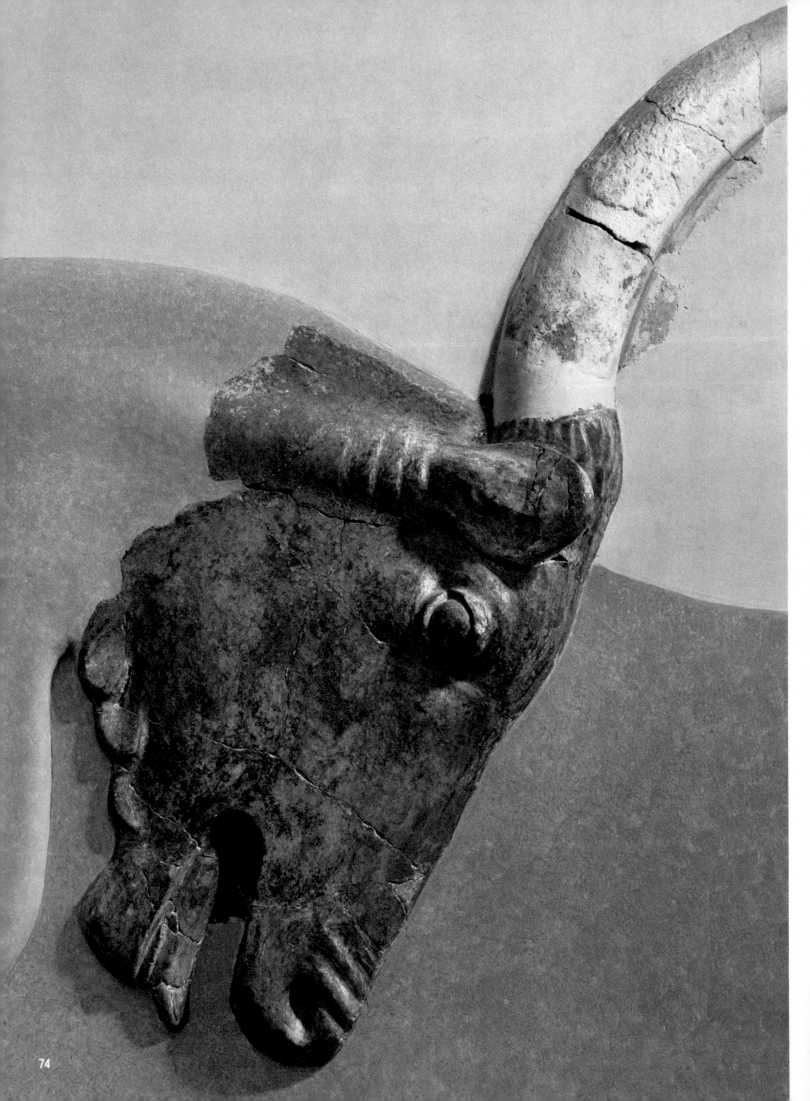

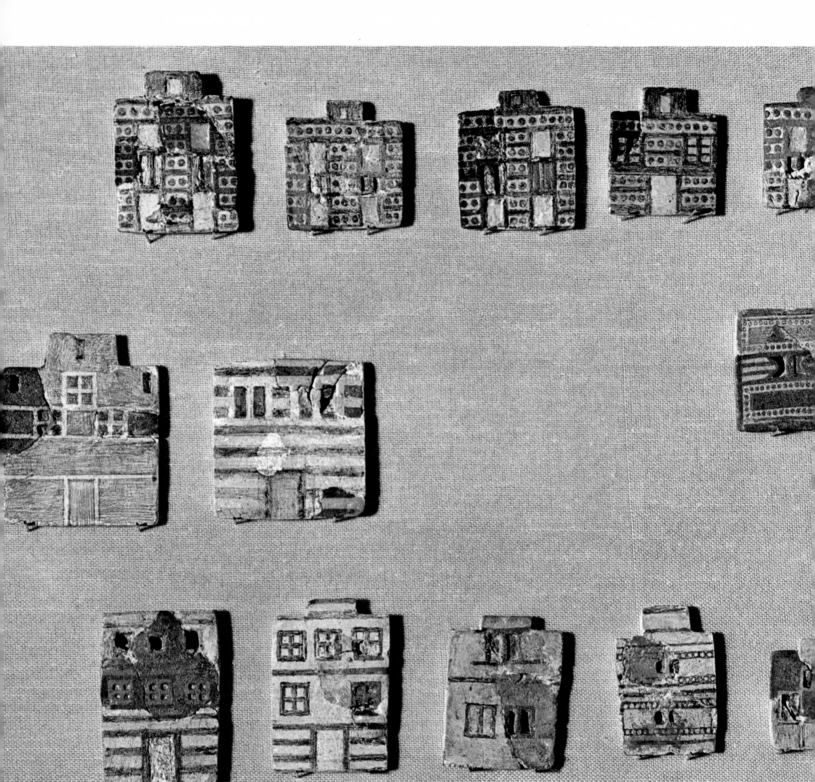

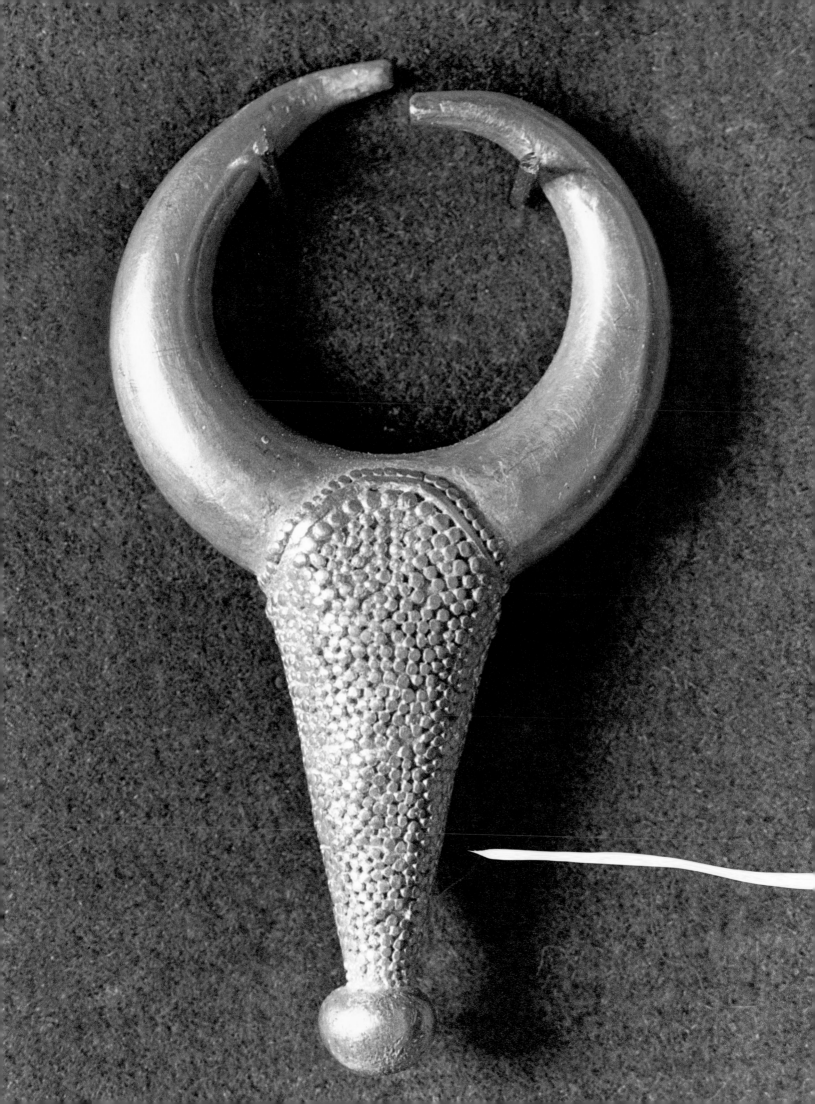

I

Ancient Knossos had two ports, one at Katsamba at the mouth of the Kairatos, the other five miles to the east at the mouth of the Karteros, which in ancient times was called Amnisos. The place is mentioned in Homer (Od. XIX, 188) in connection with Odysseus' story of a forced landing 'at Amnisos, where the cave of Eileithyia is – a difficult harbour to make'. Strabo, the much-travelled Greek geographer of antiquity, also speaks of a place Amnisos, which Minos used as a harbour. Perhaps in that long, sandy bay Theseus once landed with the Attic youths and maidens who were fated, by the casting of lots, to be devoured by the Minotaur.

From the densely-populated and prosperous harbour-town of Katsamba, ships laden with the products of the palace at Knossos, sailed into the Aegean, for the coasts of Asia Minor and Egypt. The number of its inhabitants in the heyday of the Minoan empire is estimated at several thousand. Some houses and cemeteries have been found but the development of present-day Poros and Katsamba has made further excavation difficult.

The excavations at Amnisos are very close to the shore. To the east of a small hill is a fine, two-storey villa dating back to around 1600 BC. Spyridon Marinatos found the remains of floral frescoes, the most beautiful of which shows three tall lilies (p. 97). The way in which the stems and flowers are made to stand out against a wine-red ground is highly effective. Thanks to the special technique whereby the flowers are engraved and the grooves filled in with white, a three-dimensional effect is achieved. The flower-reproductions in this ceremonial hall are arranged in a band which moves up and down by stages, thereby enhancing their appeal without disturbing the overall harmony. After the destruction of the palaces, Amnisos was resettled by Dorian Greek immigrants.

II

It was once thought that Knossos was the only palatial centre in the north of central Crete; but excavations during recent decades, more particularly in the years 1965–67, have disproved this. As long ago as 1923 Evans had uncovered the remains of a large settlement in the village of Skalani immediately to the south of Knossos, where he thought he had found a palace, and at Arkhanes, only a little farther south, he discovered further Minoan ruins. But what he assumed to be the 'summer residence of the Minoan priest-kings' had been so built over by modern houses that he was forced to abandon his excavations in the area surrounding what he described as a 'Spring Chamber'. After the country residence of Vathypetro had been discovered in 1949 at the southeastern end of Mount Juktas, the archaeologists turned their attention once again to the early discoveries at Arkhanes and the area round it. A young archaeologist, John Sakellarakis, Deputy Curator at the Heraklion museum, was entrusted with the excavations.

In the middle of this densely-populated area, he succeeded in buying a number of houses and subsequently demolishing them. As a result he was able to expose parts of a palace which, like the site at Kato Zakro, belongs to the great Minoan building period around 1600 BC. Here the most valuable find proved to be the portable stone altars (p. 98, right) which were still standing in their original position on the stylobate at the south entrance. Years earlier Evans had been made aware of these 'portable altar-bases' from engravings on sealstones and from their occurrence on the tympanum of the Lion Gate at Mycenae – where two massive lionesses are resting their paws on a slab covering two altar-bases – and so had concluded that they had some religious significance.

Even more astounding were the discoveries Sakellarakis made in October 1965 close to the village. On the Phourni hill, which stretches from the eastern slope of Mount Juktas to the valley of Ano and Kato Arkhanes, Minoan remains had already been found; at first, however, it had not been thought to connect them with Arkhanes but with a Minoan mountain-shrine on Iyttos, the name by which Mount Juktas was known in ancient times.

A cave-like hollow, which is visible from the road and which the peasants once used as a resting-place, was examined more closely and was found to be a complex tholos tomb, from the period after 1400 BC, which had partly collapsed. The first chamber had been completely stripped but behind it the excavators found a second chamber which had been walled up. Between the stones of the wall was the skull of a bull, its skeleton lying immediately in front on the floor of the first chamber. From the account of the sarcophagus of Hagia Triada (see plates on pp. 137–40) we know the relationship between the worship of the dead and the sacrifice of the bull. But never before had a bull-sacrifice actually been found in a Cretan tomb. In the narrow burial-chamber was an undamaged sarcophagus, still sealed, with a gable-shaped lid and a painted pattern which confirmed the date of the

tholos tombs (see p. 99, upper picture).

In the sarcophagus were the bones of a woman and the remains of her clothing together with some of the most valuable jewellery that has been excavated in recent years. Only a queen or a princess would have been accorded grave goods of such munificence. More than 140 individual pieces were counted, parts of necklaces, small gold rosettes which had been sewn on to the deceased's ankle-length dress, rings and two tiny caskets with lids. Of the five gold seal-rings the most important depicts a goddess surrounded by two figures and symbolic signs. Other symbols such as ritual knots and figure-of-eight shields on rings and seals suggest that this distinguished lady had in life served also as a high priestess.

Not far from the tholos tombs Sakellarakis also discovered an ossuary, which probably dates back to the much earlier pre-Palace period around 2500 BC. At an average depth of 2 feet lay 196 well-preserved human skulls, some on the ground, some in clay urns or shallow basins. In narrow compartments of this 'charnel-house', besides a number of stone vases, there were also fine ivory seals, some, for example, in the form of a button, others of a disk or a step-pyramid. Four of them bore signs from a Minoan hieroglyphic script. A unique find was a seal, used as an amulet, which consists of three superposed dice and which has no less than fourteen facets (see p. 98, left-hand picture). Here too some of the carved symbols are hieroglyphs. The excavation of the ossuary on the Phourni hill strongly suggests that, from the middle of the third millennium onwards, Arkhanes was a densely-populated and prosperous town, which, as the

queen's tomb shows, continued to be a princely residence even after the collapse of the Minoan empire.

III
The Minoan villa at Vathypetro lies not far from Arkhanes in a particularly beautiful landscape. There, at the foot of Mount Juktas, where the hills slope gently southwards to the great plain before the Asterousia mountains, a rich Minoan built his country house. As it was apparently surrounded by a considerable estate, one can assume that even 3500 years ago this whole area was under cultivation. Today the hill is surrounded by thick terraced vineyards. Not only the east wing with the foundations of a large room and a tripartite sanctuary, but also the farm-buildings are of special interest; never before had such a well-preserved winepress been excavated as here (see plate on p. 101). The pillared rooms contain many large, beautifully decorated pithoi. An olive-press, weaving accessories and the remains of a potter's kiln were also found. The building of this magnificently appointed country residence began around 1600 BC but was never completed owing to the disaster around 1550 BC.

IV
In the vicinity of one of the early Minoan towns the Nestor of Cretan archaeology, J. Hazzidakis, excavated three Minoan villas at Tylissos in the northern foothills of Mount Ida in the years 1902–1913. This town appears to have been situated on the ancient trunk road which ran along the north coast, linking the Minoan towns of east Crete with the west of the island. The houses, which belong to the Second Palace period, were not parts of a palace but detached dwellings built close

together. In these well-preserved villas, as in the traditional palace-style of planning, the entrance-halls, ritual chambers and magazines were on the ground floor – the pithoi here too under roofs supported by pillars – while the living-rooms with their terraces and verandahs were on the first floor. What purpose the three gigantic bronze cauldrons now in the Heraklion museum, the largest of which weighs 115 lb., served is a question that has never been resolved. In the view of one scholar they were used as cooking-utensils for a military unit, which guarded the Ida passes. Tylissos was a settlement long after the destruction of the palaces. Today it is a tourists' paradise, an idyllic spot in the shade of tall, dark pine trees.

Notes on the 15 illustrations that follow:

95
Ivory box from the cemetery at Katsamba (ancient port of Knossos) excavated by Stylianos Alexiou. The relief on the left shows an armed man, who is running towards the left and with his right hand is aiming a lance at an oncoming bull. Over the scene flies a large bird with outstretched wings. On the right can be seen an acrobat who has seized the bull by the horns and swung himself up in the air, as if by his own weight he hoped to arrest the animal.

96
Bronze statuette of a man (or a young god?) with pointed hat. The figure, which is only 10·5 cm. high, was found at Katsamba. The position of the arms, held stiffly away from the body with one hand on top of the other, is unusual.

97
White lilies. Fresco in a frieze from a villa at Amnisos on the north coast. The tall, graceful stems of the flowers are inlaid in white in the dark red ground, a new painting technique here encountered for the first time.

98
Left: An ivory amulet consisting of three dice with a pierced, cylindrical top, found in an ossuary on the Phourni hill near Arkhanes in central Crete. On some of the fourteen engraved facets are hieroglyphic symbols. This interesting piece dates from the First Palace period (2000–1700 BC).

Right: A quadruple stone altar from the Megaron of Arkhanes (central Crete). The pieces, which were found on the stylobate of the south entrance near a pillar, show the type of concave, curved base which had been associated particularly with the tympanum of the Lion Gate at Mycenae. These two altars are joined together under the forepaws of great lionesses, which stand to right and left of a Minoan (!) column. The same altar-design can be seen on sealstones and on one of the 'Town Mosaic' plaques (see p. 78).

99
Above: Chest-shaped sarcophagus (larnax) from a tholos tomb discovered in 1965 on the Phourni hill near Arkhanes (central Crete). In this larnax, which was undamaged and still sealed, a woman's bones and the remains of her clothing were found. The rich offerings – more than 140 individual gold beads and ornaments sewn on to the ankle-length dress, five gold seal-rings and other jewels – leave little doubt that the deceased was a Mycenaean queen or princess. The sarcophagus is painted with decorative designs of the late Minoan period: at the ends with a running spiral motif, on the front with a design which resembles the papyrus motif on the necklace at the bottom of the lower picture. The gable-shaped modelling of the lid also points to Mycenaean influence.

Below: Gold jewellery from the queen's tomb on the Phourni hill near Arkhanes (central Crete). Above the gold necklace with the papyrus motif are small rosettes, threaded together and originally sewn on to the deceased's dress. Of the five gold seal-rings at the top,

the finest specimen has a ritual scene engraved on it.

100
Minoan villa of Vathypetro near Arkhanes (central Crete). This palace-like establishment, excavated by Spyridon Marinatos, contained extensive industrial equipment such as oil- and wine-presses, a large potter's kiln and a weaving-mill. The site of the estate on a knoll surrounded by vineyards is enchanting. The building on the far side of the site is recent, having been erected at the time of the excavations.

101
Wine-press from the Minoan villa at Vathypetro near Arkhanes (central Crete), as it was found in situ. From the shallow clay vat, in which the grapes were pressed, the juice flowed into the pithos sunk into the ground below. A runnel with a stone basin was set in the paved floor. Overflow runnels of this type are frequently found in the magazines of the Great Palaces (cf. the East Magazine XIV–XX of Mallia illustrated on p. 142).

102, 103
Minoan villas at Tylissos in the northern foothills of Ida (central Crete). The villas so far excavated, which formed part of a large Minoan town, lie under the shade of broad, dark pine trees.

104
Four-handled pithos with attached bull's head (detail) from Tylissos (central Crete).

105
Two bronze votaries from Tylissos (central Crete). The two figurines, 16 and 25 cm. high respectively, represent worshippers in attitudes

of prayer with tense, arched bodies. Worship of the deity was accompanied by ritual gestures. Here the right hand is raised to the forehead in greeting – or supplication – while the left arm is held straight down. The shading of the eyes is also meant as a protection against the blinding manifestation of the divine (epiphany). Noteworthy features of the young men's dress are the mittens, soft shoes and necklace.

106
The store-room (magazines) of one of the villas at Tylissos (central Crete).

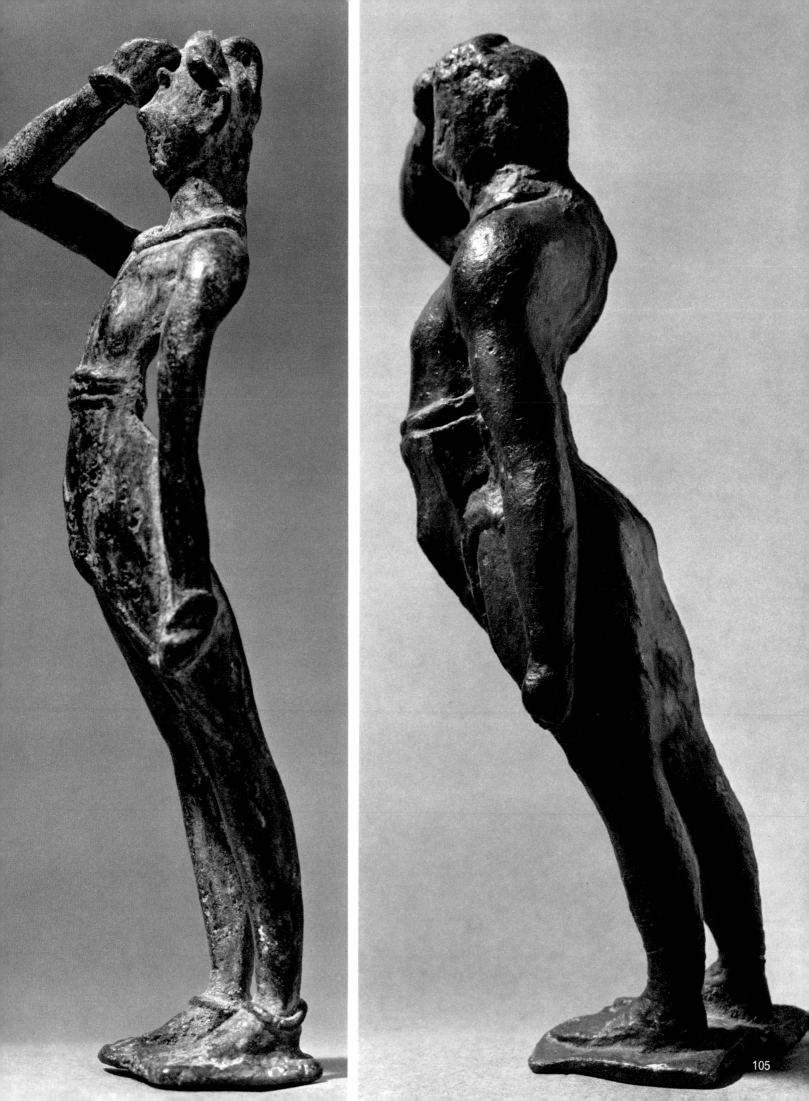

105

I

Since early Minoan times the country bordering on the fertile Mesara Plain has been one of the most densely populated areas of the island. So it is understandable that around 200 BC, when strong cultural forces were beginning to make themselves felt in central and eastern Crete, another royal residence should have been built here. As site for the new palace the easternmost outcrop of a chain of hills was chosen, which stretches from the end of the Mesara between the Ida massif and the Asterousiá mountains to the Libyan Sea. On the levelled knoll, over the remains of a Neolithic settlement, a building complex emerged, the essential components of which can still be identified.

In no other part of Crete are the ruins of the old palaces so well preserved, giving a more or less complete picture of that early period. It was indeed a regal position for a palace, overlooking the wide, fertile plain with Mount Dikte at its farthest eastern border. In the south of the island, as at Knossos, lived a family of prosperous princes – according to Greek mythology Rhadamanthys, brother of Minos, was the founder of Phaistos. From the two harbours of Komo and Matala the ships set sail for Africa and Egypt with cargoes of agricultural produce and the products of the palace workshops. By that time art and the handicrafts in Phaistos had reached their peak. The Kamares pottery – Crete never produced anything finer – was made and painted by south Cretan artists.

Adjoining West Court was the façade of the first palace. The entrance, approached by a raised causeway, lay at the court's southern end. A propylon led direct to the Central Court. Even at that time the magnificent staircases were an outstanding feature of the palace architecture. Small ritual chambers occupied the northern corner of the courtyard, which was large enough for ceremonial processions and gatherings.

The oldest building was destroyed in an earthquake but was soon rebuilt to the same plan with the addition of a wing to the north of the Central Court. This building was also destroyed by earthquakes. A third was probably destroyed by fire. All these have left their mark on the ruins. Following the general disaster of 1700 BC, the New Palace of Phaistos was built, at the same time as Knossos.

It was given a new and more ambitious look: the west façade was set back about 10 yards to make the West Court its present size. The main entrance was moved farther north close to the Grand Staircase and was embellished with broad, open steps and propylaea, which, like the great stairway at Knossos, are among the finest creations of Minoan architecture. In its final form the palace was a building of majestic proportions and in architectural beauty was more than a match for the Palace of Knossos.

Phaistos was finally destroyed between 1500 and 1450 BC in the disaster which struck all the Minoan centres. In the subsequent Mycenaean period the palace was not rebuilt, unlike Knossos where a new style, the so-called Palace Style, was actually created. At Phaistos no trace has been found either of pottery in this style or of objects bearing symbols of the Linear B script, which was deciphered as early Greek. Only the town at the foot of the hill survived the Dorian invasion and continued into the Archaic period. When the Romans conquered the island it was in turn

overshadowed by the neighbouring
and rapidly developing town of
Gortyn.

II

A unique source of information
about ancient geography is the
seventeen-volume 'Geographika'
by the classical historian and geographer Strabo (63 BC–AD 20),
whose descriptions of the island of
Crete include fairly accurate accounts of the Mesara region. He
gives, for example, the distances
between Phaistos, Gortyn and Matala. According to reports by nine-
teenth-century English travellers,
especially R. Pashley and T. A. B.
Spratt – who apparently used this
ancient 'Baedeker' as a guide – the
site of the former Minoan palace
was located where the Mesara
Plain faces the sea. The threefold
chain of hills was searched from
1884 onwards by the Italian archaeologist Halbherr, who discovered
the ruins of the palace at the eastern
end. But, as at Knossos, no systematic excavation was possible until
the end of the Turkish occupation.
Evans began digging at Knossos in
March 1900, Halbherr and Pernier
started their extensive excavations
on the palace hill in June of the same
year. The progress of the work is
recorded in the clear and carefully
compiled reports which Pernier
and, later, Luisa Banti published.
The field-work of the Italian Archaeological School is remarkable for
its sober scholarship. The authors
avoided making personal com-
ments and designated the buildings
and excavation sites with Roman
and Arabic numbers in accordance
with the two great building periods
of Phaistos, the First Palace and the
Second Palace periods. Only where
it was absolutely necessary for the
preservation of parts of buildings

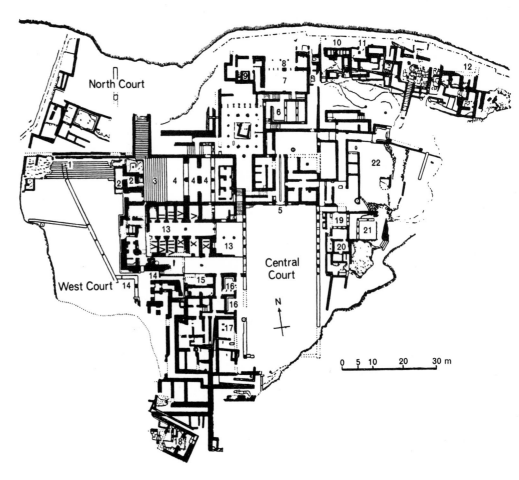

The Palace of Phaistos

1 Theatral Area
2 Ritual chambers
3 Open stairway
4 Propylaea
5 Entrance to north wing
6 'The Queen's Apartment' with benches
7 The King's Megaron
8 Colonnade
9 Ante-room and lustral area
10 'Archive', find-spot of the Disk
11 Ritual Pillar Crypt and Magazine
12 'Magazine of the Potter'
13 Antechamber and corridor of the West Magazine
14 West entrances of older palaces
15 Complex (of ritual chambers)
16 Room with wall-benches
17 Pillared room
18 Classical Temple of Rhea
19 Polythyron and light well
20 Antechamber and lustral area
21 Colonnade
22 East Court with smelting furnaces

I–XI West Magazines

was any shoring or reconstruction work carried out.

Since 1950 new and highly successful Italian excavations have been in progress under the supervision of Doro Levi; the south-western quarters of the Old Palace down the hillside and those parts of the Minoan town at the foot of the hill have been excavated, together with later buildings from the Greek and Hellenistic periods.

Also of great importance was Levi's discovery of a tholos tomb near the village of Kamilari about 2 miles south-west of Phaistos, which consists of a domed, circular main chamber and two rectangular side-chambers. Although the tomb had been robbed, ornaments of gold, stone and glass and a number of sealstones were found; there was also much fine pottery: some 500 vases and jugs and more than 1000 cups, which had contained offerings to the dead. Of unusual interest, however, are the clay offerings, which depict ritual scenes (see pp. 120 and 121).

III

The visitor to the palace now begins his tour in the elevated North Court, from which he can survey the entire excavation site. This enables him also to admire the wonderful situation of the royal residence on the crest of the hill, below which a lush tapestry of fields, olive- and orange-groves stretches away to the north, east and south. Then he descends a flight of steps to the West Court, which, with the stepped wall of the Old Palace (1), is the architectural gem of the entire building. Here, in perhaps the oldest theatre in the world, people once gathered to witness enthralling spectacles. From the open steps and the terraces of the theatre, from the North Court above and from the windows in the upper storeys of the palace, the crowd watched athletic contests, which almost certainly included acrobatic bull-leaping. This dangerous sport may have had its origins in the south of the island, where wild bulls were caught by the herdsmen. That these ceremonies in the royal palace had religious connotations is clear from the fact that in the north-east corner of the complex there were a number of small, ritual chambers (2), in which ritual accessories, offertory-plates and even an altar for burnt offerings were found.

Each of the broad steps (3) which lead up to the palace entrance is cambered. The guide explains with all the reverence due to his remote ancestors that the ruler, who walked in the middle, wanted to appear taller than those around him. A more rational explanation is that it was designed to drain off and collect the precious rain-water. Behind the steps rose the monumental propylaea (4), an entrance-doorway the beams of which rested on the thick shaft of a single column and the two antas. Passing through it, one finds oneself in the Central Court, vast, empty and very imposing. At one time the ground floor of its east and west wings was fronted by elegant pillared halls.

On the north side of the court was a central gateway (5) with two half-columns and shell-shaped niches, which marked the entrance to the north wing. This slightly more remote and isolated wing of the palace possesses, even now, a character of its own. It was here that the private rooms of the royal family were situated. The walls of the finest rooms were covered in gypsum about halfway up to the ceiling and the floors were also covered with light-coloured gypsum slabs. The interstices between the slabs were filled with red plaster, lending a colourful and decorative touch to the entire floor. The Minoan architect used this perishable material only for private rooms; the more robust volcanic limestone served for paving the courtyards. At several points in the middle of open courtyards stone basins ringed by colonnades had been erected to catch the rain-water – so the atrium and impluvium were not invented by the Romans!

As at Knossos, large pithoi containing supplies of oil and grain were found in the magazines (I–XI). Some of these vessels had different, rounder forms, while others, like the famous cups and jugs, had bright patterns painted on a dark ground.

During the summer months, when the towns and villages of southern Crete are covered by a pall of heat, the air is cool up here, for the hill is in the direct path of the north-west wind, blowing from the direction of Mount Ida. So in the olden days life was pleasant on the cool terraces, under the shady colonnades and in rooms with large folding doors which could be flung open to admit the fresh air from outside. The palace, surrounded by the dwellings of the king's subjects, was a dynamic focal point of Minoan life.

Notes on the 13 illustrations that follow:

111
The palace hill of Phaistos as seen from the plain to the south-west.

112
View across the King's Polythyron to the so-called 'Archive' in the north-east wing of the palace, where, in one of the narrow, oblong, walled-in compartments (cf. on p. 186 the repository of cult objects at Kato Zakro, which is similarly designed), the Phaistos Disk (p. 113) was found.

113
The two sides of the Phaistos Disk. Only 2 cm. thick and 16 cm. in diameter, this clay disk has impressed on either side hieroglyphs in a script which has not yet been deciphered. This runs in a spiral from the rim inwards towards the centre, and the groups of pictographic symbols are separated by straight lines. In the view of an American scholar, the symbols are a decorative variant of the Linear A script, used for ceremonial purposes. Assuming this to be correct, it would bear out the contention of those who regard the inscription as a religious text. The suggestion that the disk may have been imported from Asia Minor would seem to be invalidated by the fact that objects bearing the same symbols have been found in other parts of Crete (cf. the symbols on a double axe from Arkhalohori).

114
West front of the palace. The steps in the left foreground, the stone podium in the middle foreground and the ruined walls adjoining it, which once enclosed ritual chambers, belong to the First Palace period. The flight of steps with the propylaea behind represents the architectural peak of the new palace building. To the right, by the clump of trees, is the Central Court, which also formed part of the Old Palace. At a fairly early stage the south-east corner was damaged – possibly with parts of the palace – when a section of the hillside broke away and slid into the plain.

115
Beaked jug with reed pattern in the so-called 'Floral Style' from the New Palace.

116, 117
View from the West Court of the palace across the Central Court to the Mesara Plain. Three villages can be seen nestling at the foot of the Asterousia mountains, which form the boundary of the plain's southern end. On the far side of the mountains lies the Libyan Sea.

118
Terracotta figurine of a woman at prayer from the New Palace. The same ritual attitude with the hands held beneath the breast can be seen in the plate on p. 122.

119
View of the partly excavated Minoan town at the foot of the palace hill, as seen from the southern end of the central courtyard. The town is presumed to have stretched across to the little village of Hagios Ioannis, which can just be seen on the right of the picture.

120
Terracotta group from a tholos tomb discovered in 1958 by Doro Levi at Kamilari, about 2 miles south-west of Phaistos. The scene, representing a sacrifice to the dead, takes place in a rectangular chamber with only one wall which is broken by three horizontal windows. The figures, two standing and four sitting against the wall, are grouped round low 'altars' with sacrificial gifts. The two miniature pillars in the front corners may have supported a roof. This small funerary offering is only 16 cm. long, 10 cm. broad and 10 cm. high.

121
Terracotta group from a tholos tomb discovered in 1958 at Kamilari, south-west of Phaistos. The group shows four (probably male) figures with pointed caps, who are separated by ritual horns and are executing a dance, arms linked, in a consecrated ring-shaped area. Each figurine is about 14 cm. high.

122
Part of a terracotta figurine of a woman at prayer, Mesara (cf. p. 118).

123
Votive animals of terracotta, Mesara.

124
Landscape between Phaistos and Hagia Triada, where a palatial Minoan villa was excavated. To the north lies the Ida mountain range with the snow-capped peak of Mount Ida itself.

I

Before the Geropotamos flows into the Libyan Sea, it passes through one of the loveliest and most fertile landscapes in Crete, which, on account of its orange- and lemon-groves, is known as 'Paradise'. This also marks the end of the low range of hills of the western Mesara, on whose sole summit the Palace of Phaistos stood. The land drops by stages in a north-westerly direction towards the Plain of Tymbaki. On one of the last of the terraces, clinging to the hillside, are the remains of a Minoan villa with all the properties of a small palace.

What the Minoan name of the settlement was, we do not know. During the period of Venetian rule in Crete there was a village with 150 inhabitants, Santa Trinità, on the left bank of the river, which was abandoned during the subsequent Turkish occupation. All that finally remained was a small chapel, Hagia Triada.

In 1902, shortly after the discovery of the Palace of Phaistos, the site of the Minoan villa was found at Hagia Triada, close by the ruins of the medieval houses. Whereupon the group of Italian archaeologists who were working on the Phaistos excavation at the eastern end of the hill, started digging here too. The details of the progress they made from then until 1914 are recorded in the reports by Luigi Pernier and Luisa Banti.

Here, as at Knossos and Phaistos, relics were found from the Neolithic period. Nothing of value was discovered from the First Palace period. The villa of Hagia Triada was not yet in existence. It was not built until about 1550 BC, shortly after the construction of the New Palace of Phaistos.

There is no doubt that the villa, which has every appearance of having been a royal summer residence, had very close links with the Palace of Phaistos. This is clear not only from the fact that the two places were directly connected by a paved Minoan road but also from the nature of the building, which was constructed towards the close of the Minoan period and which conveys in an impressive manner the splendour of the kingdom.

Great care had been taken with the interior decoration of the rooms. Some were adorned with magnificent frescoes – in contrast with Phaistos, where hardly any wall-paintings were found. The floors and walls of the prince's private apartments were sheathed in gypsum. But a distinguished, cultured way of life is most powerfully evoked by the pottery which was found in the villa: the three rare steatite vessels with their relief decoration, the 'Harvester Vase', the 'Chieftain Cup' and the funnel-shaped rhyton decorated with scenes from athletic contests and bull-sports – all these, together with the painted stone sarcophagus which was found in a hollow grave on the northern slope of the same hill, are among the finest exhibits in the Heraklion museum from the peak period of Minoan culture.

II

The ground plan of Hagia Triada, which differs from that of the Minoan palace, shows a substantial group of buildings in the right-hand corner. The focal point of the complex, from which the two main wings run due east and due south, constituted the living-quarters of the prince himself; they were not only the most richly appointed but also commanded the finest views. Adjoining two main halls (2, 3) in the south was a complex of small rooms, comprising *inter alia* a living-room and bedroom (4, 5), Archive (6) and treasure-chamber (8). It was there that the most interesting finds were made. The workroom and archive, a polythyron lined with slabs of gypsum, contained not only a large number of tablets inscribed with Linear A script, but also many important seal-impressions in clay. Cupboard-like receptacles in gypsum were also found, which may have been used to store manuscripts. The small adjoining room (7) was decorated with beautiful frescoes, the finest section of which shows a wild cat stalking a pheasant. To the east lay the magazine (8) in which ingots of crude copper weighing 65 lb. each were stored. These so-called 'talents', which were also found at Kato Zakro, are the earliest form of currency. The ingots were officially weighed and stamped with a royal hallmark.

Of the rooms mentioned earlier, the living-room (4) is still remarkably well preserved. From comfortable wall-benches, which run the length of the gypsum-lined walls, one can look through the open hall (3) and the large reception-room (2) at the countryside beyond. To the north lies a large terrace (1) with a magnificent view of the river, the mountains and the sea, which in those times doubtless came up to the hill. Just as the rooms on the north side of the Palace of Phaistos caught the fresh breeze that blew from Mount Ida, so these rooms also had the benefit of the fresh north-west wind that came in from the mountains and the sea.

Towards the southern end of the residential wing lay the staff living-quarters (10) and several workshops and magazines. It was in one of these rooms that the 'Chieftain

The Villa of Hagia Triada

1 Open terrace
2 Main hall with pillars
3 Portico
4 Room with wall-benches
5 Bedroom
6 Workroom and Archive
7 Room with frescoes
8 Treasure-chamber with 'bronze talents'
9 Pottery store
10 Staff quarters
11 Minoan road
12 Corridor and magazines
13 Late Minoan water-conduits
14 Family living-quarters
15 Great Court of the Sanctuaries (Piazzale dei Sacelli)
16 Hagios Georgios Galata
17 Steps to eastern exit
18 Late Minoan sanctuary
19 Staff quarters
20 'Minoan village'
21 Late Minoan market

ABCD Mycenaean Megaron

126

Cup' was found (see p. 130). The main magazines, however, were in that part of the villa which lay beyond the slowly-ascending north causeway. Some of the many pithoi found there are lavishly decorated with reliefs. In this part of the villa, which stretched as far as the South Court, extensive alterations were made in the Mycenaean period. A massive and, it seems, megaron-type building (ABCD) was constructed here over the ruins of the royal villa. The South Court itself (15) dates from the same period as the Minoan villa. As the excavators found a remarkable quantity of votive offerings on the site, they called it the 'Piazzale dei Sacelli' or 'Great Court of the Sanctuaries'. Most of the objects found were terracotta figurines of men and women with strange features, and of animals, but the most original was a model of a Minoan ship. In the south-western corner of the court, near the steps leading to the chapel of Hagios Georgios Galata (16), lay the shattered funnel-shaped rhyton decorated with scenes of athletic contests (see pp. 132 and 133). On the eastern fringe of the court was a Minoan road leading to the east exit of the villa. The plate on p. 131 shows the broad, shallow steps leading up to it (17).

In the northern sector of the excavation, on the terrace below the north causeway, is a part of the building which is much more Mycenaean in style than Minoan. On the left side of a road which today runs down under the shade of pine trees to the river below lies the 'Minoan village' (20), foundations of houses from the Late Minoan and

the most part, after the villa was destroyed.

III

Finally, if one climbs up the hill behind the remains of the Agora, one very soon reaches the area where the inhabitants of this place, throughout the centuries, buried their dead. There are two burial-places here (cf. p. 29) which are amongst the oldest on the island. Influenced by the North African style, they were built in the round, and the inward-sloping walls seem to suggest that they were originally covered by some kind of dome. All round these two circular tombs lay the cemetery of the later Minoan periods, to which the painted sarcophagus from the stone-faced rectangular grave, the prize exhibit of the Heraklion museum (see pp. 137–140), also belongs. The stone sarcophagus, which is painted on all four sides, dates back to about 1400 BC and therefore to a period in which the rulers of Knossos and indeed the South as a whole were Greeks of Mycenaean origin. Nevertheless the scenes depicted appear to be of Minoan funeral rites.

The centre-piece shows the sacrifice of a bull, whose blood runs into a vat (p. 137). On the opposite side of the sarcophagus women can be seen carrying containers, the contents of which – presumably blood of the sacrificed bull pour into a larger vessel o shape. One can assur officiating person is at the far end. He a long robe

are seen approaching him with sacrificial gifts in the form of two young bulls and a boat.

A definitive interpretation of these scenes is not possible, as no explanatory text is available. All one can say with certainty is that objects appearing in these paintings, such as bull, tree, bird, double axe and priestess, are essential to the Minoan religion, whereas other scenes, particularly those depicted on the ends of the sarcophagus (p. 140), introduce us to an entirely strange world. The most striking example of this is the horse and chariot, which only became an appurtenance of Cretan aristocratic society in the Late Minoan period.

THE VILLA OF HAGIA TRIADA

Notes on the 13 illustrations that follow:

129
View of the excavated site of the Minoan villa at Hagia Triada. The western end of the Mesara Plain is a particularly fertile area, full of orange and lemon trees, which is popularly known as 'Paradise'. Through the centre of the picture winds the Geropotamos ('old river'), which continues to flow summer. Passing through the of Tymbaki, it flows into Gulf of Mesara. The two mountains i

stretched hand. His long hair hangs down to his belt, jewellery adorns his neck and arms, and he wears boots (or are they leggings laced over shoes?) and an apron. The figure on the left has a shouldered sword and is wearing a plumed helmet. He is more simply clad and has very little jewellery. It has been suggested that these figures, usually described as 'prince and officer', could also be children acting the parts. This elegantly-shaped goblet has a beautiful girdle-pattern round the base and the rim; a similar pattern is used vertically to separate the scenes depicted on either side.

131
Flight of steps leading to the east exit of the villa of Hagia Triada and the paved Minoan road, which ran along a hilly ridge to the Palace of Phaistos.

132
Bottom register of a funnel-shaped rhyton in black steatite from the villa of Hagia Triada. This detail shows a long-haired young man, without helmet, knocking his opponent down in a boxing-match.

133
Second register of the rhyton reproduced on p. 132, showing an acrobat flinging himself backwards over the head of a bull and apparently being gored. The other two registers show a display of wrestling and pugilism by men wearing helmets.

134–136
The 'Harvester Vase', a black steatite rhyton shaped like an ostrich-egg from the villa of Hagia Triada. Most experts believe that it represents a group of agricultural workers returning home. The men, who are marching in pairs, are led

by a bare-headed man dressed in a quilted jerkin and carrying a long stick over his right shoulder (p. 136). The implements carried by the other men could be threshing-flails or poles with which to knock down olives. The sickle-shaped knives or hooks attached to shafts are a curious feature. One man is singing lustily (p. 134) and swinging a rattle (sistrum). The realism of the scene is enhanced by the backward-turned head of one single man (p. 135). To present such an animated scene in a curved relief band only 7.5 cm. high calls for remarkable artistry. In some quarters it has been suggested that these are soldiers carrying harpoons, but this interpretation is not widely accepted.

137
Painted stone sarcophagus from a chamber tomb near Hagia Triada. One side of the sarcophagus, showing a bull being sacrificed. Three women in ankle-length dresses walk behind a man playing a double flute. The sacrificial bull, whose blood runs into the vat on the ground, is bound to a table by red ropes tied crosswise, and under the table lie two goats, also possibly intended for sacrifice. The priestess on the right is busy at the altar. The jug and fruit-bowl may also represent sacrificial gifts. On the extreme right of the scene a sacred tree appears above an altar decorated with ritual horns.

138, 139
Details from the other side of the stone sarcophagus from Hagia Triada. Women in long dresses, followed by a lyre-player, are carrying buckets on a yoke over the right shoulder (p. 138). The scene, which is painted on a light background, continues farther towards the left, where it shows the liquid – pre-

sumably the blood of the sacrificed bull – being emptied into a two-handled vessel standing between two ritual symbols. Moving in the opposite direction from the centre to the right – this time against a dark background – are three men clad in skirts of hide. They are bringing two oxen and a boat to a herm-like figure who is wrapped in a hide mantle. Beside this figure a tree is growing close to a wall with steps. On the extreme right stands a high altar. The background for this portion is once again white.

140
The ends of the stone sarcophagus of Hagia Triada, each showing a chariot; one is drawn by dark horses, the other by fabulous animals with brightly-coloured wings. The figures holding the reins can be identified as women by their white complexions.

I

Between the northern foothills of
the Dikte range and the Sea of Crete
lies a broad coastal plain, which
terminates in the wide, shallow
Gulf of Mallia. On the eastern
fringe of the plain the Minoans
established a settlement, which,
thanks to a number of favourable
circumstances, grew to a considerable size. It occupied a key position
on the north coastal road between
east and central Crete; as trade with
the Aegean islands and the Near
East developed, it became an important transhipment-port. In the
centre of this town, which covered
about half a square mile, a palace
was built around 2000 B C.

The Minoan names of the settlement, the palace and the ruling
family have not survived; we have
only the authority of Greek legend
that Sarpedon, brother of Minos
and Rhadamanthys, was king of
the third Minoan royal residence.
The modern name Mallia has no
Minoan root but comes from the
Greek 'omalos', 'omalion', which
means 'flat', 'levelled' and refers
to the character of the coastal landscape.

The disaster of 1450 B C struck
both town and palace: the tidal
wave from the volcanic eruption of
Santorin hit the coastal settlement
head-on and overwhelmed it.

II

Towards the end of the last century,
when a herdsman found some gold-
leaf near the sea, the local inhabitants started digging for Minoan
treasure. J. Hazzidakis, the ephor of
Cretan antiquities, began systematic
excavations in 1915. They were
continued with the support of the
Ecole Archéologique Française
d'Athènes, and between 1921 and
1932 excavation of the palace was

completed. At the same time work
had been proceeding on the site of
the town. The West Court was
excavated in 1960, and work has
since continued on the western and
southern quarters as well as on the
ruins of the town between the
palace and the sea. The French
archaeologists have published the
results of their investigations in
their *Etudes Crétoises*. They too
have decided against reconstructing
entire sections of the palace. As at
Phaistos, concrete and iron sup-
ports have been employed only
where they were necessary to pre-
serve the Minoan buildings. Protective roofs were erected over the
most important sections of the
excavation.

At Mallia few Neolithic remains
were found; a few tombs from the
pre-Palace period were discovered
near the sea. The north-western
parts of the palace excavation defin-
itely date back to the construction
of the Old Palace around 2000 B C.
A cemetery in the vicinity of the
oldest of the tombs belonged to the
Middle Minoan town. Because of
the gold ornaments that were found
there (cf. the pendant on p. 148), it
has become known as Chrysolakkos or Pit of Gold. The lay-out of
the New Palace, built after the
disaster of 1700 B C, has all the
characteristics of a typical Minoan
palace, except that there is no
monumental theatral area. Mallia
also has fewer rooms than Knossos
and Phaistos, and none of them
has the splendid gypsum lining.
Only the local sandstone and limestone were used.

III

A paved road led from the town to
the main entrance in the north (1).
There are two large, multi-handled
pithoi with rope and spiral designs

to act as sign-posts for the present-day visitor (pp. 150–151). Passing the magazines (I–VI), one enters the North Court (2) and the 'Tower Court' (3), the name given to it by the archaeologists when they uncovered a square structure (4) with very thick walls. To the south lies a pillared hall (6) with ante-room (5) and beyond that the Central Court.

Open colonnades on the north and south sides provided a splendid setting. Behind the east wall of the court are storerooms (XIV–XX), which, to judge by the gutters in the floor, were used to store oil. In the middle of the vast Central Court stands an altar for burnt offerings (eschara) (7), the only one to be found in such a position. It stands exactly opposite the middle of the ante-room (8) of the Pillar Crypt (9), one of the ritual chambers in the west wing. This consists, as at Knossos, of a number of consecrated and public rooms. An interesting architectural feature is the so-called 'Loggia' (10) which on its north side adjoins the staircase (11) leading to the first floor. It was presumably from this open hall, which projects slightly over the courtyard, that the king appeared before the assembled multitude on ceremonial occasions. That it was an official room was confirmed by the important finds made in the room (12) behind the 'Loggia'; the head of a sceptre in the form of a panther (p. 148), a dagger and a large sword with a gilded blade and a pommel richly ornamented with crystal and amethyst. Also within the sacred precincts of the west wing is the circular sacrificial stone (kernos) (13) in the south-west corner of the courtyard (p. 149); the hollows round the edge were perhaps designed to take offerings of first-fruits and seed. Behind the rooms along the west

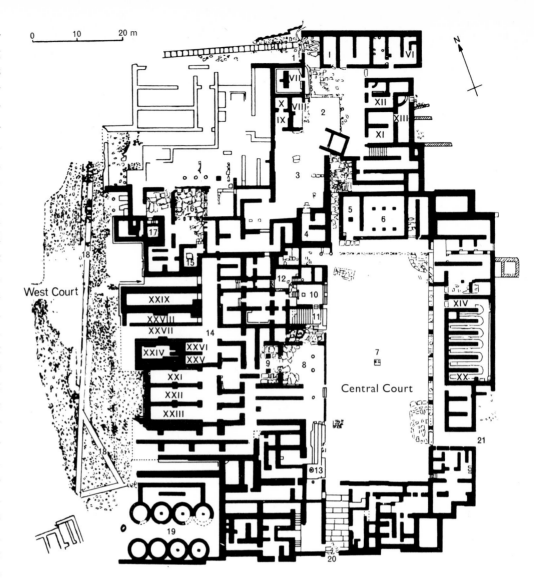

The Palace of Mallia

1 North entrance
2 North Court
3 Tower Court
4 Tower
5 Ante-room
6 Pillared hall
7 Altar for burnt offerings
8 Ante-room
9 Pillar Crypt
10 'Loggia'
11 Staircase to upper storey
12 King's private room
13 Kernos
14 Corridor of West Magazines
15 Room with pillar
16 Polythyron and columned hall
17 Lustral area and ante-room
18 Processional Road
19 Grain silos
20 South entrance
21 South-east entrance

I–VI	North-east Magazines
VII–X	Workshops and magazines
XI–XIII	Magazines
XIV–XX	East Magazines
XXI–XXIX	West Magazines

façade of the courtyard ran the corridor of the West Magazines (14), a lay-out very similar to that of Knossos.

Leaving the palace on the west side, one passes through its oldest part, which included one of the king's private apartments (15), a polythyron (16) and a lustral area (17). Then, in front of the orthostat base of the Old Palace, the paved West Court opens out. Across it, from north to south, runs the so-called 'Processional Road' (18). It forks at the south end of the courtyard, the left fork leading to two groups of four circular containers (19), each built round a central pillar. Presumably these were not water-cisterns but grain-silos.

As the ruins of the palace were left in the state in which they were excavated, one has an uninterrupted view of the beautiful landscape surrounding them. This is what gives Mallia its particular charm. The palace and the town are spread out, wide and flat, in a fertile green plain, which stretches away to the bare, brown slopes of the mountains and to the sea, a clear blue line behind the Central Court. The contrasts of colour are particularly striking when the sun rises behind the spit of land that juts into the sea or in the evening when its slanting rays fall on the reddish-brown ruins and pour their fading light into the chapel of the Profetes Elias on the hill on which the mountain sanctuary of the Minoan town once stood.

IV

The Gulf of Mirabello, at the point where Pachyammos lies today, has been since very early times a much favoured landing-place for mariners and traders, who were able to transport their cargoes across the island where it is narrowest to the south coast and thereby avoid the arduous and often dangerous voyage round the eastern tip. This may have been one of the factors that led to the foundation on the north coast of Gournia, which must have been a prosperous town around 1600 BC. We have no precise information about its relations with the great palace-centres in the west. Its prosperity naturally derived to some extent from the wealth of the Minoan palaces, but it seems to have lived a life of its own as an independent community. When the Minoans lost their power, it too declined. People forgot where it had been situated, forgot even its name.

About the turn of the century, when the great era of excavations began, the town was discovered by the American Harriet Boyd-Hawes. Its network of streets and closely-packed rows of houses cover the entire hilly ridge, at the top of which a small 'palace' with adjoining Agora stood in a slight depression. Among the objects found in the very small rooms of the houses in the town, many of them two-storeyed (cf. plate on p. 78 and note), were domestic utensils and implements, which their owners had not had time to move when disaster struck the town.

V

The island of Pseira in the Gulf of Mirabello, which today is uninhabited, waterless and barren, once had a prosperous Minoan port. The English archaeologist Richard Seager excavated it in 1907. The fine pottery and the colourful stucco reliefs, which recall those of Knossos, testify to the high living-standard of this settlement. In view of its strategic position, it may well have been administered by Gournia and used as a customs-post in the gulf.

VI

A further indication of the density of the Minoan settlements in eastern Crete is Palaikastro, which lay in a sheltered bay on the east coast not far from Sitia and grew into an important town. Excavations by English archaeologists in the years 1902–1904 revealed that this settlement pre-dated the construction of the Old Palaces. Finds such as the 'Shepherd Bowl' (see p. 41) and a series of interesting votive offerings in the form of figurines and female heads from the sanctuary on Petsofa hill reveal the high standard of that early art. After the disaster of 1450 BC the town was rebuilt and in the Archaic period, as Heleia Chora, it acquired special importance as the site of a sanctuary of Diktaean Zeus. The stele bearing the inscription of a hymn to Zeus Kretagennes, who was born in Crete, is in the Heraklion museum. This hymn was sung by youths at the spring festivals to celebrate Zeus' birth. Armed with shield and spear, they performed the same wild dances which the Curetes had performed about the infant Zeus in order to drown the child's cries with their clamour (cf. note on plate 224, p. 216).

*Notes on the 18 illustrations that
follow:*

145
Part of a pithos with spiral and
banded design from the New Palace
at Mallia.

146, 147
View of the King's private rooms
in the north-west wing and the
Central Court behind, in the centre
of which (extreme left of photograph) stands an altar for burnt
sacrifice (eschara). Visible on the
hillside to the right is the Elias
chapel occupying the site of the
former Minoan sanctuary.

148
Above: Gold pendant in the form
of two hornets sucking at a drop of
honey, from the Chrysolakkos
tomb at Mallia (about 2000 BC).
The small disk in the centre with the
fine granular design shows at what
an early stage the Minoan craftsmen
had mastered the art of soldering
tiny gold grains.

Below: Sceptre-head of grey slate
in the form of a panther, the body
tapering off to form the cutting
blade of an axe: from the earliest
stage of the New Palace of Mallia.

149
Round ritual stone (kernos) *in situ*,
in the south-west corner of the
Central Court. It was presumably
used to offer various seeds and
first-fruits to the deity.

150, 151
View across the paved Minoan road
to the north entrance of the palace.
The multi-handled pithos on the

right dates back to the First Palace
period. The relief-work with which
it is decorated seems to be a reproduction of the network of cords
which was necessary to transport
these giants.

152
Gournia, the Minoan town situated
on a ridge overlooking the Gulf of
Mirabello. On the extreme right,
in the distance, can be seen the
shimmering white houses of Hagios
Nikolaos on the opposite shore.

153
Late Minoan bath-shaped sarcophagus from Pachyammos near
Gournia. The fish painted on the
inside and the presence of an outflow
hole suggest that it was originally
used as a bath-tub.

154
Late Minoan bath-shaped sarcophagus from Gournia with paintings of a cow giving suck and of a
calf.

155
Cobbled Minoan road in the upper
part of the town of Gournia.

156
Rhyton with dolphins from the
island of Pseira (east Crete).

157
The island of Pseira in the Gulf of
Mirabello (east Crete), which pos-
sessed a Minoan port-settlement.
This was excavated in 1907 by
British archaeologists.

158
Two pithoi from the island of
Pseira (east Crete). The ritual vessel
on the left is decorated with the
heads of oxen and double axes with
slender olive-branches between.

159
Vessel in the form of a two-handled
carrier-bag decorated with double
axes, from the island of Pseira (east
Crete).

160
The Bay of Palaikastro (east coast).
The Minoan town lay to the right
of the Kastri crag, which juts out
into the sea. The ancient name of the
town is not known. It and Gournia
were the most important Minoan
urban settlements on the island,
Palaikastro being the more prosperous of the two. The hills in the
middle distance rise to a point,
880 feet up, where the Minoan
sanctuary of Petsofa stood.

161
Clay chest-like sarcophagi (lar-
nakes). The larnax in the foreground
is from Palaikastro (east Crete) and
has slightly recessed panels on which
double horns and a winged griffin
are painted. The entire sarcophagus,
including the lid, is covered with
ornamentation. The gable-shape
points to the period of Mycenaean
influence from the mainland.

162
Late Minoan casket (pyxis) in alabaster with pierced lugs in the shape
of small shields – from Sitia (east
Crete).

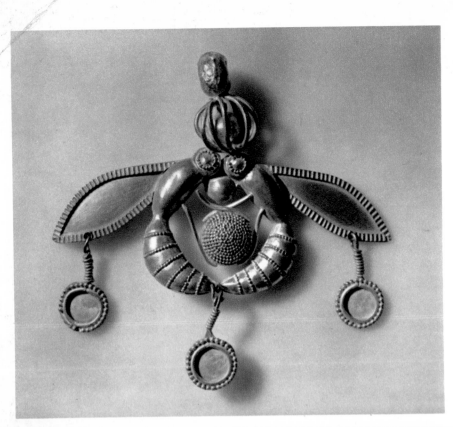

153

154

159

The successive discoveries of the great Minoan palaces of Knossos, Phaistos and Mallia confirmed the archaeologists in their view that at a very early stage in Crete's history there had been several royal residences, each a seat of government for a specific region of the island and each with direct access to the sea. The precise number of these centres, from which the brilliant Minoan culture sprang, was not known. But scholars were agreed that one day still further Minoan sites might well be discovered. There were compelling reasons why increasing attention was paid to the eastern part of the island, for archaeological research had already revealed a series of large villas, a Minoan hill-sanctuary with numerous votive offerings to the Mother Goddess, and several cemeteries. Did it not seem logical to assume that such a concentrated manifestation of Minoan art must have had a focal point in a palace?

Various indications pointed to Kato Zakro, a bay roughly halfway down the east coast. After a trial dig in 1961, which lasted only a few days, the real archaeological excavation began the following year with a team of scholars, technicians and skilled workers, of which I was in charge. It is financed by the Greek Archaeological Society in Athens and by an American couple, Leon and Harriet Pomerance, who have a passion for antiquity. Systematic excavations are proceeding; but already such exciting discoveries have been made as to exceed even our wildest hopes. The Minoan town covers two ridges which run along the side of a small depression. Vines and olives grow in abundance almost down to the beach of the small, well-protected bay. One of the many streams from the mountains

of Ano Zakro flows in leisurely fashion down to the sea. It forms a great loop round the southern of the two hills, on the summit of which the picturesque chapel of Hagios Antonios stands out, dazzling white. Approaching from the north, one passes through the barren, mountainous country at the eastern end of the island. At Ano Zakro the road descends along a deep gorge, the walls of which are pitted with the dark shadows of caves. As they once served as burial-places, we called this gorge the 'Valley of the Dead'. The remoteness of this particular region would hardly have recommended it as a site for a palace. But it has been established that Kato Zakro was the most important naval base in Minoan Crete, as well as playing a major role in trade with Asia Minor and Egypt. Shipping conditions at that time were such that a base of this kind was essential. The raw materials – copper, bronze, ivory and gold, together with hard and rare types of stone – were shipped into the port of Zakro, while the products of the highly-developed Minoan industry were exported to the great markets abroad. Some of these masterpieces can be seen in the hands of Cretan envoys – Keftiu – on the frescoes in Egyptian tombs. From the same port Minoan ships laden with long cypress-trunks set sail for the Aegean and brought back cedarwood from the Lebanon. The sheltered bay was a refuge for ships in distress. And finally Zakro was the base from which the ships protecting the Minoan thalassocracy maintained their control of the eastern Aegean.

Before the excavations began, the bed of the valley was covered with rubble and boulders with only the occasional patch of cultivated land where vines, bananas and olives had been planted. Peasants, tilling their fields, had come upon squared blocks of ashlar and the stone base of a fairly large column. But no visitor would have dreamt at that time that relatively near the surface lay the extensive ruins of a Minoan palace. Yet the signs were already unmistakable: we had barely started digging when we came upon foundations and before long the royal chambers emerged, one after the other, fully furnished just as when the catastrophe 3500 years before had engulfed them. So far over an acre with more than 70 rooms has been excavated. We have reason to suppose, however, that the entire area covered by the palace was twice as large. At a reasonably conservative estimate the original building, which was at least two storeys high, covered some two acres and comprised between 250 and 300 rooms. Clearly Zakro is not of the same magnitude as the labyrinthine Knossos but, when it has been fully excavated, it will almost certainly compare with the two other palaces, at Phaistos and Mallia.

The general layout of Zakro resembles that of the other Minoan palaces. There are two main and two lesser blocks, each of two or three storeys, grouped round a rectangular central court. The palace was extended westwards by the addition of an outside block. Each room communicated with the next as in a labyrinth. Several flights of steps led to the upper storeys. The internal planning of the palace blocks was functional. The fact that some rooms were used only for ritual purposes indicates that the great Mother Goddess was also worshipped at Zakro. But there are distinctive constructional features which go to show that Minoan architects were not content merely to follow in the footsteps of more illustrious predecessors. To any architectural problem they would find a solution which, while naturally depending on the exigencies of the site and on the wishes of the client, also provided scope for artistic talent. This was the case at Zakro. Unfortunately we are not in a position to reconstruct the original plan of the building. The natural catastrophe which literally razed the palace to the ground made that impossible. Added to that the intervening centuries have also wrought great havoc, and the cultivation of the soil over the ruins has done further irreparable damage. This is particularly true of parts of the palace in which sections of the floor had actually been exposed. So the casual visitor will find it difficult to gain an impression of the former size and splendour of the palace buildings. Only the archaeologist, who can compare it with the other palaces and who can visualize each fresh detail as it is uncovered – however unimportant it may seem – in the context of the whole, will be able to reconstruct in his mind's eye this complex building as it originally was. We were fortunate, when we came to excavate the fourth Minoan palace, in being able to draw on the experience gained from a century of archaeological research into Aegean prehistory. Moreover, since the period of great archaeological discoveries at the beginning of the present century, considerable technical progress has been made and the equipment at the archaeologist's disposal has greatly improved.

It is not possible for me in the space at my disposal to give a detailed description of the site at Zakro and of the rich finds we made there. Nevertheless, with the help of a few representative photographs and a ground plan, which shows the state of the excavations at the end of 1966, I will try to give the reader a picture of this Minoan palace, the treasure-chambers of which yielded a harvest of rare works of art that further testify to the artistic genius of the Cretan people. Some of these finds are unique of their kind – not even at Knossos has their like been found. And no less extraordinary is the large amount of pottery – up to the present no less than 3500 vases have been found! – which may be attributed to Kato Zakro having been the only palace in the Creto-Mycenaean world which was not robbed after the disaster.

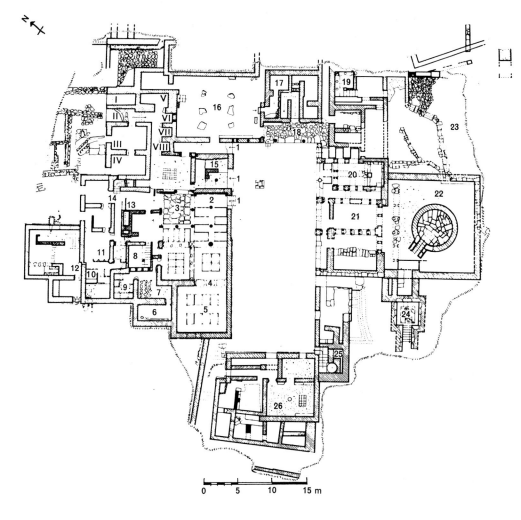

The Palace of Kato Zakro

  1 Approaches to the West Block
  2 Reception room with polythyron and columns
  3 Open court
  4 Tripartite door
  5 Dining-room
  6 Magazine for small pithoi
  7 Workroom
  8 Lustral bath
  9 Treasure-chamber with caskets
10 Lavatory
11 Archive
12 Storeroom for raw materials
13 Store of 'talents' and elephants' tusks
14 Staircase from workshops to upper floor
15 Propylaeum opening on to the Central Court
16 Kitchen
17 Kitchen quarters
18 Ante-room to private apartments
19 Lustral bath with ante-room
20 Queen's Megaron
21 King's Megaron
22 Square room with central basin
23 North-east approach
24 'Spring-chamber' (artificial spring)
25 Well with wooden windlass
26 Southern store-room and workshop area

I–VIII West Magazines

The main approach to the palace was from the sea (23) but as yet neither this road nor the main entrance to the palace has been excavated. It remains to be seen whether Zakro also had propylaea at the entrance of the same majestic proportions as in other palaces, more particularly Knossos. A second approach-road from the south linked the palace with the southern quarters of the town, which extended over the slopes of the Hagios Antonios hill (p. 181). The houses, which had several rooms and relatively high storeys, were ranged along steep, paved alleys and flights of steps. Entering the great Central Court, one was confronted by the four high plain façades of the palace blocks. The façade of the West Block was faced with carefully-hewn blocks of tufa and had three wide doors (1), which were doubtless ornamented, and a row of double windows. The special feature of the wall on the east side of the court was a series of stepped passages flanked by pillars and columns, which formed a small pillared hall on the ground floor. This portico was surmounted by a verandah on first-floor level. The north front of the court gave access to the private apartments, which one entered through a sort of reception-room (18), an ante-room with two columns. This wing of the palace rose in terraces up the side of the north hill. On the south side of the Central Court a wide opening led to a separate block of buildings.

The most instructive way of embarking upon a tour of the palace is to enter the public rooms in the West Block, by crossing the monolithic threshold of one of its three great doorways (1). The one on the left led into the first of the reception-rooms (2), beyond which lay a small paved court surrounded by columns (3), which acted as a light well. The timbered ceiling was supported by an inner row of columns. A series of adjacent folding-doors (polythyra) enabled the room to be subdivided when required. The floors of this court and of the adjoining room were covered with a special material – a Minoan 'plastic' – hitherto unknown and possibly a by-product of resin, and they were decorated with individual red stucco designs in meander and rectangular patterns. A tripartite door (4) led into the next room (5), the walls of which were decorated with a frieze of running spirals in low relief. This room presumably served as a dining-room, as ten amphorae for wine and eight smaller jugs were found there. At the bottom of the megaron light well – having probably fallen down from the upper storey – lay two of the most valuable finds made at Zakro: a libation vessel (rhyton) of steatite in the form of a bull's head (p. 180), and a second, egg-shaped libation vessel in hard stone on which a Minoan mountain-sanctuary is depicted (p. 192). High up on the lintel of a great entrance-doorway decorated with a spiral design sit four young wild goats in pairs facing each other, attendant on the invisible (aniconic) Mother Goddess. Other 'agrimia' – 'agrimi' is the name of the wild goat which is still to be found in Crete – are depicted on the rhyton: one animal stands with its forefeet on a rock (p. 194), while another is fleeing in terror (p. 193). Birds of prey hover around or sit on the tips of great ritual horns, which crown the sanctuary. In the courtyard in front of the doorway there are three different kinds of sacrificial altar.

Immediately behind the public rooms in the West Block are the smaller rooms of the so-called 'Sacred Precinct'; they can be identified by the sacral niches and the low stone bench. A very large number of libation vessels (rhyta) in terracotta were found here. Another room, in which a high sacrificial table stood, contained sacred objects and ritual vases. In the same area was the lustral bath (8), to which one descended by a short flight of steps. On the floor of this bath lay a magnificent vase of veined marble (p. 190). The bold, imaginative design of the two large handles, which beginning at the middle of the vessel curve round to meet the upper of the two rims, makes it one of the most beautiful vessels in the palace. The objects consecrated to the worship of the goddess were found on the floor of one chamber (9) in chest-like containers, which are divided into compartments by partitions of unpolished tiles coated with plaster (p. 186). Wonderful things came to light in these chests: a complete collection of the most beautiful vases in alabaster, veined marble, basalt, red marble and other kinds of stone, tall libation chalices (pp. 189 and 191) of such remarkably contrasted workmanship that it is difficult to believe they are made of even harder material, for example of mottled obsidian, a crystalline volcanic rock. A particularly fine and rare piece is the small rhyton of rock crystal (p. 187). Its elegant handle is made of crystal beads which were held together by a bronze wire. Amongst the other objects found were water-jugs and ritual alabaster jugs, delicately fluted vessels, ritual hammers in coloured marble which were employed as sacred symbols, faience vases moulded into the shape of a bull's or lioness's head and, finally, large bronze double axes. One of the largest is covered with finely incised floral motifs.

In the same area of the palace is the Archive (11). Here clay tablets inscribed in Linear A as well as in the Minoan language were found; they had been preserved in individual niches. A particularly interesting discovery was a storeroom (12) containing piles of raw materials. The magazines in the West Block (I–VIII) were situated partly in the cellars, where the great earthenware storage-vessels (altogether 50 of these giant pithoi were found) stood along the walls. Amphorae were used to store wine; they were fitted with a number of handles and magnificently ornamented with floral motifs or with all kinds of fish, or simply with spiral designs. Other magazines were used for storing smaller vessels such as jugs, cups, beakers and bowls, almost all of which are delicately and elegantly ornamented. Six copper ingots (so-called talents), each weighing 65 lb., had fallen from a magazine on the first floor to the ground floor (13). They had been imported from the island of Cyprus, while four enormous elephant-tusks, for the production of ivory objects, had come from Syria. Various ivory objects were found in the palace. A large room in the North Block seems to have served as a kitchen and dining-room (16). The ceiling was supported by six wooden columns, the bases of which we were able to excavate. That this must have been used as a kitchen would seem to follow from the fact that the bones of large and small animals, whose flesh had been cooked, were discovered here. An enormous cooking-pot was still standing on the ashes in the fireplace. Two of the small adjoining rooms (17) were full of cooking-pots and kitchen utensils. The Minoan palace kitchen at Zakro is the first to have been found complete with equipment.

The West Block had been extended to accommodate workshops. One of these was a dye-house, where the liquid colours were produced in a row of tubs. Kato Zakro appears to have specialized in murex-fishing and dyeing. On a small island near by a large number of snail-shells were found with manufactured violet dye. So in all probability the Phoenicians learned their famous handicraft from the Minoans of east Crete! A staircase (14) leads from the workshops to the first floor, which was connected by three other staircases with the upper floors of the West Block.

The royal apartments were discovered when the East Block was excavated. In the usual Minoan style these were designed as megara with light wells and a polythyron – a continuous series of doors. Nevertheless they too differ in certain particulars from the palaces known hitherto. For instance, adjoining a series of private apartments (20, 21) there is a square room (22) – one enters it through a polythyron – in the middle of which is a cistern, a sort of swimming-pool, with spring-water still bubbling out of it (p. 184). Eight steps lead down to the basin, which was originally colonnaded. Two of the bases of the columns are in the basin itself, while a third was found near by. Two other carefully designed springs were found on the south side of the great square room. Eleven steps led down to one of them (24), while the other was reached by way of an underground passage. A well with a flight of eight steps was situated in a room (25) in the southern corner of the palace. It had been fitted with a wooden windlass. At the bottom a number of small dishes were found, which had contained various foodstuffs. It must be assumed that the occupants of the palace, horror-stricken at the disaster which had befallen them, had thrown these down as votive offerings to the goddess. One dish contained olives, the pulp of which had been remarkably well preserved by the water. A room (19) in the north-east sector of the palace had been designed as a bathroom but had later been turned into a lustral bath, as there were frescoes on the walls showing ritual horns. Its special features were the gypsum benches and the short, slender columns on high pedestals.

In the South Block a second complex of magazines and workshops was discovered (26). In one of the magazines large quantities of domestic utensils were found, particularly kitchenware and vessels for storing solid and liquid supplies: jugs, casks, amphorae, buckets and cooking-pots – one three-legged pot stood out because of its extraordinary size – cooking-ovens, hotplates, sieves and the like. Some of these objects were in bronze. In one workshop rock crystal had been used; pieces of it lay around, some in the crude state, others already partly worked. There were also pins with knob- or mushroom-shaped heads. Stone vases were also produced here. Some magnificent pieces were found, amongst them a particularly fine red marble lamp decorated with a wreath of leaves in low relief. Fragments of faience vessels found in the workshop on the floor above show that another form of handicraft was practised there; this workshop also yielded a triton shell superbly carved in stone.

The palace extends towards all four points of the compass. Large parts of it still lie hidden under the ground. As the finds can be exactly dated, it has been established that the Palace of Zakro was built in the sixteenth and early part of the fifteenth century BC, that is, in the Second Palace period of Knossos, Phaistos and Mallia. Zakro was also destroyed at the same time as the other three. The disaster that struck the island was totally unexpected. The earth tremors were so violent that entire walls of squared stone blocks and burnt tiles were dislodged before they crashed in ruins. The earthquakes were followed by fire, which reduced the palace and the surrounding town to rubble and ashes. In the opinion of Marinatos, the destruction of the Minoan palaces was a direct consequence of the great volcanic eruption of Thera (Santorin) about 1450 BC. As the island burst open and the greater part of the volcano's crater was flooded, a gigantic tidal wave resulted, which swept over the Cretan coast opposite Santorin. Large tracts of country along the coast were buried under a shower of ash. Marinatos's theory has been borne out at Zakro, where the excavations revealed huge lumps of volcanic debris which had been flung across during the eruption, a distance of some 80 miles! That the eruption was preceded by earth tremors seems clear from the fact that in many rooms stonemasons and carpenters had left behind their tools – for example, about ten long saw-blades. After the first tremors, the people had immediately set about repairing the damage. The account of the explosion of Thera, which had been recorded in the archives of an Egyptian high priest, later found its way through the agency of Solon, into Plato's Dialogues between Timaeus and Critias, as an account of the destruction of the legendary island of Atlantis.

Notes on the 28 illustrations that follow:

171

Above: Gold dish with spiral decoration, formerly in the Giamalakis Collection. The central rosette also occurs in the diadem reproduced in the lower picture and in the gold pendant (pp. 172 and 173).

Below: Gold diadem, formerly in the Giamalakis Collection. In the centre stands the goddess as 'Mistress of Animals' with outstretched arms holding two wild goats by the hind-legs. The remainder of the gold band is covered with spiral designs in which two octopuses are framed.

172, 173

Gold pendant in the form of a bull's head, formerly in the Giamalakis Collection. This fourfold enlargement brings out the masterly embossed work and the particularly beautiful spiral rosette which suggests the curly hair on the forehead. The fact that this very motif was employed in all three pieces of jewellery (cf. also p. 171), indicates that they were made in the same workshop. The pendant, dish and diadem were all found by a peasant while he was tilling his fields at Kato Zakro and he gave them to the collector Dr Stylianos Giamalakis, of Heraklion. As soon as their Minoan origin was established, excavations were started at the spot where they had been found, with the result that the fourth Minoan palace was discovered.

174

Narrow-necked jug with handle. This elegant vessel, which is painted all over with swimming argonauts, may have come from the same workshop as its double, now in the Musée Borély in Marseilles.

175

East Cretan landscape between Palaikastro and Ano Zakro.

176

Stirrup jug with running spirals over an arcade motif. The flat handle very close to the narrow neck, so designed to allow the liquid to emerge only in drops, is characteristic of a style that gradually replaced the rhyton in eastern Crete.

177

The 'Valley of the Dead', a gorge between Ano Zakro and Kato Zakro; in its steep walls a number of burial niches and caves were found.

178

Nine-handled pithos with octopuses, murex snails and corals in the East Cretan Marine Style.

179

Mouth of the 'Valley of the Dead' in the coastal plain of Kato Zakro.

180

Bull's-head rhyton in black steatite (horns restored). Somewhat smaller than the famous libation vessel of Knossos (p. 70), it is also an outstanding piece of craftsmanship, for example in the reproduction in relief of the curly hair, which covers most of the bull's forehead.

181

View from the Hagios Antonios hill in the south-west across the palace excavation. In the foreground are the southern quarters of the Minoan town. Beyond the cypresses stretches the western part

with workshops, magazines, 'sacred precinct' and public rooms (covered in dark green foliage), which border on the Central Court. To the north of it, in rising terraces, are the great kitchen and dining-room with the royal private apartments to the right.

182, 183

View from the northern slope across the palace excavation. Between the magazines in the right foreground and the Central Court on the extreme left are the rooms of the 'Sacred Precinct' with treasure-chamber and lustral bath as well as the courtyards and rooms of the West Block. The west façade facing the Central Court was built on a foundation of carefully-hewn square blocks of tufa. On the east side of the Central Court can be seen the circular outline of the large palace cistern.

184

Above: Ritual vase with twin 'figure-of-eight' handles.

Below: Large palace cistern east of the Central Court. Eight steps lead down to the pool, which was originally surrounded by a colonnade and in which the spring water still bubbles up.

185

Rhyton with starfish, murex snails and corals.

186

Above: A double axe incised in the north wall of the palace. There are many such symbols on the pillars of the sacred precincts in the great palaces (e.g. in the crypts of Knossos). They are symbolic of the worship of the invisible ('aniconic') deity. In the Palace of Phaistos, apart from the double axe, there are also ritual symbols for tree, plant, trident, shears, etc.

Below: The treasure-chamber of the palace at the south end of the West Block. The walls of the individual compartments, which are made of rough tiles covered with plaster, have been partly restored. In the 'repositories' lay many objects consecrated to the Mother Goddess, such as rare vases and tall vessels (libation chalices) of alabaster, marble, basalt and obsidian (see pp. 189 and 191).

187
Rhyton of rock crystal from the repository for ritual treasures. The crystal beads forming the handle were held together by a bronze wire. Particularly beautiful is the crystal ring with gilded faience 'bracelets' round the neck of the vessel.

188
Alabaster cup with handle.

189
Ritual chalice of veined marble from the repository for ritual treasures. The bowl of this quatrefoil chalice has very thin walls.

190
Amphora with handles in grey-white veined marble with dark red patches, from the lustral bath next to the treasure-chamber in the West Block. This fine vase with its boldly-designed handles is one of the most beautiful of the vessels found at Kato Zakro. Previously this form of vase had only been found on seals and wall-paintings.

191
Left: Ritual beaker in veined marble with horizontal grooves from the treasure-chamber in the West Block.

Right: Ritual beaker in black obsidian with crystalline speckles from the treasure-chamber of the West Block. Obsidian, a volcanic rock, is a particularly hard material; it was used for tipping spears, for making knives and saws and was imported from the volcanic islands of Melos, Thera and Yali (south of Cos).

192
Egg-shaped rhyton in stone. This find, the most important of the entire excavation, gives us the clearest picture so far of a Minoan hill-top sanctuary, which is identified as such by the 'horns of consecration'. Above the doorway with its spiral design four wild goats with great horns keep guard, and a bird of prey hovers over the sacred horns; below the doorway an altar stands in the open, and the ritual horns appear over brick walls and on lintels. This rhyton can compare in importance with the three previously-discovered relief vases of Hagia Triada (see pp. 130, 132–136).

193
Wild goat in flight in mountain country. Reverse of the relief rhyton on the opposite page (detail). Fragments of gold leaf show that the vessel was originally gilded.

194
Wild goat standing on rock. Reverse of the relief rhyton on p. 192 (detail).

195
Above: Head of a wild goat. Votive offering of painted terracotta. The wild goat – 'agrimi' in Cretan – roamed the uninhabited mountains of east Crete. Today it is only to be found in the great gorges of the White Mountains in west Crete.

Below: Mouth of gorge known as the 'Valley of the Dead'. During the excavations a tomb was found intact high on the left-hand wall of the gorge; it contained valuable votive offerings from the pre-Palace period, e.g. vessels in the Vasiliki Style (see p. 31) and a flat steatite box with a recumbent dog on the lid as a handle, corresponding exactly to the pyxis lid illustrated on p. 34.

196
Above: Stone butterfly with decorated wings, which may originally have been part of a casket.

Below: Double axe of ivory. The double blades are very rare. Another example found at Kato Zakro was a richly engraved double axe in bronze, which lay in the repository for ritual treasures.

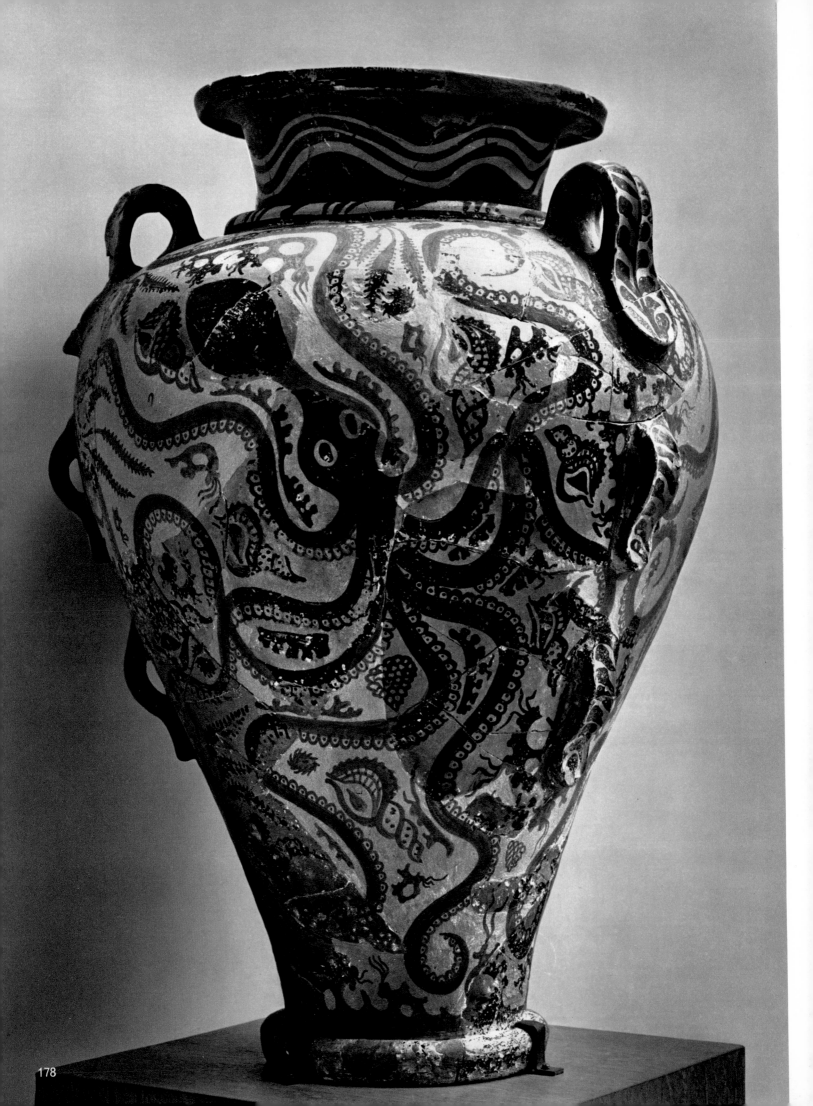

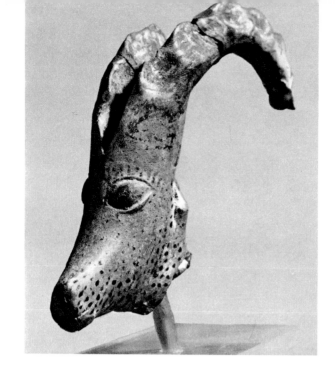

The New Palaces at Knossos, Phaistos, Mallia and Kato Zakro were all destroyed as a result of a devastating catastrophe which must have taken place around 1450 BC at the earliest. Marinatos's view, that the volcanic eruption of Thera (Santorin) set up a tidal wave which engulfed the settlements on the northern coast of Crete only 80 miles away, has become more and more widely accepted, especially since the excavations at Kato Zakro revealed deposits of volcanic debris which had been hurled across the sea. The simultaneous destruction of such centres as Phaistos and Hagia Triada or Vathypetro and Sklavokampos in the interior of the island is less easy to explain. But as such natural disasters are invariably accompanied by earthquakes, these places may well have been destroyed in the same way.

The Palace of Knossos alone survived among the Cretan palaces – and it was the only one to come to life again. Pottery in the 'Palace Style', of which Knossos is the only known source, provides concrete evidence that the arts continued to flourish. At other places in the island, for example on the ruins of Hagia Triada and of the town of Mallia, buildings were constructed which reflect the growing influence of a non-Minoan people, the Achaeans from the Greek mainland. In the course of that century the Greeks of the Peloponnese had become sufficiently powerful not merely to challenge the authority of the Minoans in the Aegean but even to threaten Crete itself. The Achaeans flocked to the island in droves, settled there and spread their Mycenaean culture. This is confirmed in particular by the discovery in tombs near Knossos of objects which had their counterparts on the Mycenaean mainland. Ever since these discoveries were first made, the nature of the Greek settlers' influence upon Crete has been a source of lively discussion among archaeologists.

A study of the works of art of that period, however, leaves no doubt that, in spite of the increasing domination of Knossos by the Achaean Greeks, the age-old Minoan artistic heritage managed to survive. The old Minoan worship persisted with astonishing obstinacy and continued to express itself in the traditional forms. One example is the tomb on the Phourni hill near Arkhanes (cf. p. 92 and notes for plates on p. 99), which dates back to the period around 1350 BC. The woman buried in the sarcophagus not only held a high social position at the time of her death but also performed the functions of a priestess. The Mother Goddess, the idol of womanhood, is still the focal point of worship. The finest evidence of this is the series of ritual representations of female figures from this period. The largest and most interesting goddesses were found in country districts such as Gortyn and Gazi and on the Karphi hill, where such traditions as the hands uplifted in benediction – which can be traced back to Neolithic times – could be preserved right up to the end of the post-Palace period. The idols stood in consecrated rooms in private houses, some of them still in their original place on stone benches along the walls. Their attributes remained the same: snakes, birds and ritual horns.

That other influences were also at work is clear from the two bronze statuettes (p. 199), in which one can see the first signs of the Geometric Style. And in the small clay model of a temple, even although it is round (p. 213), one can see the beginnings of Greek influence. The idol in the shrine is still a goddess with raised hands, but she is seated and is guarded by two men, who look down on her through an opening in the roof.

THE POST-PALACE PERIOD

Notes on the 16 illustrations that follow:

199
Left: Bronze statuette of a votary from Grivigla near Rethymnon.

Right: Ram-bearer in bronze formerly in the Giamalakis Collection. By contrast with the two votaries from Tylissos (p. 105), 200 years earlier in date, whose arched bodies express great inner tension, the bodies of these two men are erect and tranquil. This is particularly noticeable in the figure on the left, which has an almost military stance. The right hand is no longer raised to the forehead in a gesture of worship. The long hair falls in stylized locks over breast and back. Both figures are forerunners of the approaching Geometric period.

200, 201
Painted terracotta statuette ('kourotrophos') from the Mavro Spelio cemetery near Knossos. From a short cylindrical base emerges the bust of a woman holding her child up in front of her. Dating from 1350 BC, this figure, which presumably represents the Mother Goddess, is, so far as we know, the oldest of a long series of idols with such a cylindrical base.

202
Painted terracotta group of dancing women with a lyre-player in the middle, from Palaikastro (east Crete). Dances in which the participants form a ring are still to be seen in Crete, a relic of the dance which Theseus performed as he led the Attic youths and maidens through the winding labyrinth back to freedom. This momentous occasion in the palace of Minos is still celebrated in the Tsakonikos, a dance from the southern Peloponnese.

203
Votive figurine from Gournia in painted terracotta. The figure, with right hand held to the temple, is seated.

204
Female idol from a shrine near Gortyn in the Mesara (detail). The goddess wears a spiked diadem, above which snakes' heads appear, signifying that she is a goddess of the underworld.

205
'The Poppy Goddess'. Female idol from Gazi near Heraklion. Three poppy-seeds have been inserted in her crown to signify that she is the goddess of fertility and healing. The symbol of the poppy is also to be attributed to the goddess of sleep and death. This idol was found, together with four others (see pp. 206 and 207), in the consecrated room of a house. All the idols have their hands raised in the same solemn attitude and are wearing cylindrical jackets. They are among the largest and most interesting examples of female divinities from the post-Palace period.

206, 207
Female idols with crowns of doves and ritual horns from Gazi near Heraklion (cf. plate on p. 205).

208, 209
Female idols from the post-Minoan settlement on the Karphi hill above the Lasithi Plain (east Crete). The headdress of the goddess on the left consists of three doves over a disk-diadem; the figure on the right is wearing a crown decorated with doves and large disks. Dainty feet peep out from under the bell-skirt.

210, 211
The Lasithi Plain in east Crete: View from the Diktaean Cave of Zeus across the fields of the densely-cultivated plain, which is irrigated by several thousand wind-driven water-wheels. In the background, rising above the white-walled village of Tzermiadha, is cone-shaped Karphi ('the nail'), on which a post-Minoan town of considerable size was excavated. (cf. the idols on pp. 208 and 209).

212
Female figure with snakes from a shrine near Gortyn in the Mesara. In addition to the snakes' heads over the diadem, the goddess has snakes coiled round her arms and hands.

213
Small clay model of a round temple from Arkhanes (central Crete). Inside the shrine, which is fitted with a door, sits a goddess with raised hands. Two men are watching the figure through a chimney-like opening in the roof. Above the door is a recumbent animal.

214
Tree with seven birds. Painted terracotta from a grave at Fortetsa near Knossos.

201

The Dorian tribes, which moved southwards from north-western Greece to the Peloponnese around 1200 BC and, armed with iron weapons, destroyed the strongholds of the Mycenaean princes, did not stop there but spread through the southern Cyclades until they got to Crete. The conquest of the island was no peaceful infiltration. Thanks to their military superiority, the Dorians occupied the archaic Minoan settlements and built their strongpoints on mountain terraces and hilly plateaux along the north coast, from the Gulf of Mirabello in the east to the extreme west.

The Dorians put an end to the old, over-refined Minoan civilization and imposed their social system on the conquered people. As in Sparta, only the Dorian aristocracy enjoyed political rights. The peasants became serfs, while the urban population, though subject to military service, retained their individual freedom. Towns, not unlike city-states, led an independent existence: Gortyn, for example, had its own laws. The island, which at that time enjoyed a fresh period of economic prosperity, also reached a new peak of artistic achievement in the so-called 'Daedalic Style'.

Notes on the 14 illustrations that follow:

217

View of the Acropolis from the Agora of the Dorian town of Gortyn (Mesara). Embedded in the hillside between the cypress trees lies the still unexcavated Greek theatre. Gortyn only came into its own after the destruction of Phaistos, when it developed into the most important Dorian settlement in southern Crete and around 500 BC codified its own municipal laws (see pp. 218–219). Its seaport, Leb-

ena, was extremely popular as a spa and place of pilgrimage to the shrine of Asclepius which was built over the mineral spring.

218

The 'Municipal Laws' of Gortyn. The text of the laws, formulated in 500 BC, is inscribed on blocks of stone and gives one an insight into the contemporary legal and social structure of Dorian society. Civil and criminal laws, for example, define family rights, the property and hereditary rights of married couples, the purchase and maintenance of slaves and land-ownership. There is no doubt that this legislation did not apply solely to the town of Gortyn. The Romans built the Greek tablets into the walls of their Odeum. In the year 1884 the Italian archaeologists Halbherr and Fabricius found twelve of the twenty tablets near the bed of the ancient River Lethaios and built protective masonry round the stone wall. It is the longest Greek inscription so far discovered. The laws are drawn up in an ancient Doric dialect. The script follows a zigzag course in the so-called *ordo bustrophedicus*, which means, as the ox ploughs the furrow, from left to right and again to the left, with the result that the letters in the second line appear as in a mirror.

220

Relief group from the Acropolis of Gortyn (Mesara). Two of the three naked deities are depicted in front view with their hands pressed against their thighs. The central figure is presumed to be a male god. The strong oriental influence on Cretan art during this period is unmistakable here. The limestone relief is in the so-called Daedalic Style (800–650 BC), which is regarded as the forerunner of the

Archaic Style. Its Cretan origin is implicit in the name. Daedalus, who is said to have invented both the sculptor's tools and the art of monumental sculpture, also plays an important part as a mythological figure, for example as the builder of the labyrinth at Knossos. The many discoveries that were made on the Acropolis at Gortyn underline the importance of this art-style.

221
Athena from the Acropolis of Gortyn (Mesara). Terracotta. The position of the arms suggest that the goddess was carrying spear and shield.

222
View of the hill north of the pass leading into the Mesara Plain, on which the Dorian hill-town of Rhezenia once stood. On the strongly fortified Acropolis two Archaic temples (mid seventh century BC) were excavated.

223
Enthroned goddess from the inner doorway of the Archaic temple A of Rhezenia (central Crete). The austere attitude of the goddess is characteristic of the orientalizing style. She is fully clothed and her skirt has incised animal patterns. Entering the temple from the pronaos, the worshipper passed through an inner doorway, over the lintel of which was an architrave. At either end of it were identical, seated statues of the goddess, facing inwards. Under their feet was an elaborate relief of lions and stags. One is inevitably reminded of the Minoan 'Mistress of Animals'.

224
Bronze shield from the Idaean Cave. On the eastern slopes of Mount Ida, above the 4500-foot-high Nida Plateau, lies the cave to which the pre-classical and classical tradition gave great prominence as the birthplace and retreat of Zeus. The finds made here – the cave is by far the richest source of Cretan bronze objects – point to the existence of a cult of the Curetes, in which dancing with shield and spear formed an important part. There are a number of splendid shields with artistically decorated central bosses, but one in particular depicts a dramatic scene of Zeus fighting with wild beasts and flanked by two (winged?) Curetes beating gongs.

225
View from a point below the Dorian hill-town of Dreros (east Crete) looking towards the town's harbour at Olous. The harbour settlement once lay where nothing more than the narrow isthmus between the gulf and the lagoon (see note on plate 231) is now to be seen.

226
View of the hillside near the village of Aphrati, where the Dorian town of Arkades once lay. Situated to the west of Mount Dikte, it must have been a prosperous town to judge by the variety and quality of the objects found here. The sculpture, in particular, is remarkable for its portrayal of human features.

227
Dorian half-relief from Arkades.

228
Group of hills with the remains of the town of Praisos (east Crete). Built by the Minoans who had fled from the invading Dorians into the mountains at the eastern end of the island, it eventually became the capital of the so-called Eteocretans, the 'real Cretans', a section of the population which, by virtue of its geographical isolation, succeeded in preserving Minoan customs and religion and even the Minoan language for a considerable time. Fragments of Eteocretan inscriptions have been found at Praisos, which are written in Greek letters in the *ordo bustrophedicus* but have not yet been deciphered.

229
Lion couchant from Praisos.

230, 231
View from the hillside of Dorian Aptera, looking down on Suda Bay, with the Akrotiri Peninsula near Khania (west Crete) beyond. This was the site of one of the earliest Dorian settlements and, when Gortyn was at its peak, was the most important trading town in west Crete. Greek legend has it that a musical contest once took place between Muses and Sirens, in which the Sirens were defeated. In despair they tore off their wings and plunged wingless ('aptera') into the sea; hence the two small islands.

232
Quarry near the Dorian port of Phalasarna (west coast). A great submarine movement, the precise date of which is not known, caused the western end of the island to be lifted out of the water and this artificial harbour belonging to the hill-town of Polyrrhenia was created. At the same time the port of Olous disappeared in the Gulf of Mirabello (see note for plate 225).

POSTSCRIPTS

Nearly all of the photographs in this book were taken by me in the Spring of 1966. I am indebted to Professor Max Hirmer for those reproduced on pages 32, 53, 101 and 148; to Mr John Sakellarakis, Deputy Curator at the Archaeological Museum in Heraklion, who excavated Arkhanes and the cemetery on the Phourni hill, for those appearing on pages 98 and 99. The book virtually owes its inception to the Editor of the monthly magazine *Du*, who commissioned me to go to Crete in order to photograph the masterpieces of Minoan art. The issue in question, which appeared in January 1967, met with such success, that I was tempted to undertake an illustrated book on the same theme, using a number of hitherto unpublished pictures. I owe a special debt of gratitude to the publishers for producing the work in so handsome a manner.

For permission to photograph the works of art my grateful thanks are due, not only to the responsible officials at the Ministry in Athens, but in particular to Dr Stylianos Alexiou, the Director of the Heraklion Museum. His key contribution on the development of Minoan art affords my pictures the necessary art-historical backing. I am greatly indebted, too, to Professor Nikolaos Platon, firstly for allowing me to photograph both the site of Kato Zakro and the objects found there, and secondly for his valuable account of the dramatic laying bare of this, the fourth Minoan palace.

I should like to thank my friend Nikolaos Metaxas, of Heraklion, for allowing me to photograph for reproduction in this book several hitherto unpublished pieces in his comprehensive art collection.

The driving force in this project was provided by Mrs Hanni Guanella, of Zurich, whose tireless zeal greatly facilitated my work. In Crete I placed myself in her trustworthy hands; in the building up of the book she became my indispensable collaborator, who contributed the bulk of the narrative text and all the notes on the plates.

LEONARD VON MATT

Collaborating with Leonard von Matt on the present book was a welcome continuation of our joint work on the January 1967 issue of the magazine *Du*, which was entirely devoted to ancient Crete.

In order to ensure that the photographs would make the maximum impact upon the viewer, thus enabling him to appreciate to the full the remarkable achievement of the Minoan artists, we considered it best to use a chronological framework for this book. In accordance with the now generally accepted chronology, the material is divided into four main categories: the pre-Palace, First Palace, Second Palace, and post-Palace periods. The closing section on Dorian Crete deals briefly with the invasion of the island by the Greeks.

I would like to take this opportunity to express my very special thanks to Dr Alexiou, the Director of the Archaeological Museum in Heraklion. He freely gave of his time in order to run through the pictures and the text, making constructive suggestions and pointing out inaccuracies, thereby rendering an invaluable service. In my analysis of the palaces at Knossos, Phaistos and Mallia, I was in large measure guided by his book on Minoan Culture. No less helpful were Professor Platon, Mr Sakellarakis and his wife, the excavators of Kato Zakro and Arkhanes/Phourni.

Not wishing our book to take on the aspect of a 'museum guide', we occasionally allowed ourselves to depart from the strict chronological treatment, which enabled us to illustrate the countryside in which the works of art had their origin. This gave rise to the introduction of monographs, such as those on Knossos, Phaistos, and Kato Zakro, or descriptions of a particular region, such as that around Knossos, or the eastern part of Crete. In this way the south Cretan landscape of the Mesara Plain with Mount Ida as back-drop is conjured up when a Kamares vase is presented to the viewer, while a sight of the east Cretan landscape evokes the priceless treasures of the latest Minoan palace to be excavated, that of Kato Zakro; in short, the salient features of this island of Crete, with whose culture and scenic beauty it would take a lifetime to become fully acquainted, come a little more clearly into focus.

HANNI GUANELLA

233

SELECT ANNOTATED
BIBLIOGRAPHY

BOWMAN, J. *Crete*, London, 1962. A reliable guide, containing useful information not only about ancient Crete but also about later periods, and the island's present-day traditions and customs.

DEMARGNE, J. *Aegean Arts*, London, 1964. A detailed description of the Minoan and Mycenaean civilizations, profusely illustrated, and indicating their contribution to the basic elements of classical Greece.

EVANS, SIR ARTHUR *The Palace of Minos at Knossos* (4 vols. in 7), London, 1921–36, photographic reprint New York, 1964. A well documented and very detailed account of Minoan-Mycenaean civilization based on the author's excavations begun at Knossos in 1900.

GRAHAME, J.W. *The Palaces of Crete*, Princeton, 1962. A clear and well-arranged study of the palace and house architecture of the great age of the Minoan civilization in the sixteenth and fifteenth centuries BC (LMI and II). It discusses the origin of the Cretan palace and analyses it. Useful for the student and tourist.

HIGGINS, R.A. *Minoan and Mycenaean Art*, London and New York, 1967. A survey of the Minoan and Mycenaean cultures and the Cycladic from shortly before 3000 BC to the Dorian invasions. Includes detail on manufacturing methods.

HOOD, S. *The House of the Heroes: The Aegean before the Greeks*, London and New York, 1967. A concise but very good introduction to the subject, though controversial in parts.

HUTCHINSON R. W. *Prehistoric Crete*, Harmondsworth and Magnolia, Mass., 1962. Useful supplement to Pendlebury's *Archaeology of Crete*, covering the whole field of Cretan archaeology from the earliest times to the sixth century BC. Contains a great deal of information obtained at first-hand.

KENNA, V.E.G. *Cretan Seals*, London, 1960. Combined catalogue of the Minoan seals in the Ashmolean Museum, Oxford, and a general conspectus of the art of seal-engraving in Crete in the Bronze Age. The only study of Cretan seals in English.

MARINATOS, S. *Crete and Mycenae*, London and New York, 1960. (Photographs by M. Hirmer). A standard work, characterized by excellent black-and-white and colour plates, by an archaeologist who has done important excavation work in Crete.

MATZ, F. *Crete and Early Greece*, London and New York, 1962. An introduction by one of the leading German scholars in the field.

PENDLEBURY, J.D. *The Archaeology of Crete*, London, 1939 (reprint New York, 1965). Still a standard work, summarizing and collating previous results. It includes much material not previously published and the author's own excavations.

—— *A Handbook to the Palace of Minos and its Dependencies*, London, 1935, reprinted London and Chester Springs Pa. A practical guide to the intricacies of the Knossos complex by a co-worker of Sir Arthur Evans.

PLATON, N. *Crete*, London and New York, 1967. A survey of Minoan civilization written within the context of the author's 30 years' work in Crete. A separate section analyses the art and civilization by subject, not chronologically.

REVERDIN, O. *Crete in Colour*, London and New York, 1962. (Photographs by R.E. Hoegler). Outstanding colour plates, providing a wide coverage of the Cretan scene. There is a section on Cretan flora by Professor N. Creutzburg.

FAURE, P. *Fonctions des Cavernes Crétoises*, Paris, 1964. A special volume on cave exploration which contains the most complete bibliographical record of the literature on Crete, from ancient sources up to the present time. Valuable not only for the speleologist but for all who wish to learn about earliest Crete, when the caves were still sacred places where the inhabitants worshipped Eileithyia, or the Great Mother Goddess, and Zeus, who was born on Crete.

TIRÉ, C. and EFFENTERRE, H. van *Guide des Fouilles Françaises en Créte*, Paris, 1966. A concise account of these major excavations, indicating the original reports for fuller details.

ZERVOS, C. *L'Art de la Créte néolithique et minoenne*, Paris, 1956. The classic work on Minoan art, with excellent photographs of pre-Minoan and Minoan objects clearly documented. Now out of print and difficult to obtain.

LEVI, D. *Gli scavi a Festós negli anni 1958–1960*, and in *Annuario 39–40, 1961, 62, 1963*. Official record of the excavations at Phaistos.

PERNIER, L., and BANTI, L. *Il Palazzo Minoico de Festós*, 1935 and 1951; *Guida degli scavi Italiani in Creta*, 1947. Both by the Italian archaeologists who excavated Phaistos and Hagia Triada.

SCHACHERMEYER, F. *Die ältesten Kulturen Griechenlands*, Stuttgart, 1955. The picture section of this book on Aegean prehistory ends with illustrations of the earliest Cretan pottery.

—— *Die minoische Kultur des alten Kreta*, Stuttgart, 1964. A comprehensive study of Minoan antiquity, clearly narrated and profusely illustrated.

ALEXIOU, S. *Minoikos Politismos* (Minoan Culture, Greek text) Heraklion, 1965. The most important up-to-date publication on recent excavations on the island by the Director of the Heraklion museum. In addition to providing a succinct survey of the various periods of Minoan civilization, this book contains detailed accounts of the excavations at Knossos and Mallia.

—— *The Minoan Goddess with Raised Hands*, (Greek text) Heraklion, 1958. Of particular interest for the study of the Minoan post-Palace period.

Key:
AMH   Archaeological Museum, Heraklion
MET   Metaxas Private Collection, Heraklion
L   Length   l   left
B   Breadth   r   right
H   Height   c   centre
D   Diameter   a   above
                        b   below

23	Diktaean Cave	AMH	L 5 to 11 cm
25	Koumasa	AMH	H 23·5 cm
26	Koumasa	AMH	H 23·6 cm
28	Mesara	MET	l H 10 cm
			r H 18 cm
31	Vasiliki	AMH	H 34 cm
32	Mochlos	AMH	l H 7·2 cm
			r H 12 cm
33	Mesara and east Crete	MET	D 4·5 to 8 cm
34	Mochlos	AMH	D 14 cm
36	Maronia	AMH	D 17 cm; H 11·5 cm
37	Mochlos	AMH	L 7 cm; D 3 to 3·5 cm
38	Mochlos	AMH	H 18 cm
41	Palaikastro	AMH	D 19·5 cm
42	Koumasa	AMH	L 20·5 cm; H 15 cm
43	Koumasa	AMH	H 18 cm
44	Petsofa	AMH	H 17·5 cm
45	Kapetaniana	MET	H 8·5 cm
46	Vorou	AMH	L 74 cm; H 21 cm
47	Eastern Mesara	MET	H 75 cm; D 50 cm
50	Mesara	MET	l H 25 cm
			c H 27 cm
			r H 18 cm
51	Old Palace, Phaistos	AMH	H 27 cm
52	Old Palace, Phaistos	AMH	H 69 cm
53 a	Old Palace, Phaistos	AMH	H 16·2 cm
53 b	Old Palace, Phaistos	AMH	l H 5 cm
			r H 7·5 cm
54	Old Palace, Phaistos	AMH	H 55 cm
66	New Palace, Knossos	Knossos	H 1·38 m; base 90 cm; B 62 cm
67	New Palace, Knossos	Knossos	D 90 cm; H 20 cm
68–69	New Palace, Knossos	AMH	H 29·5 cm
70	New Palace, Knossos	AMH	H 15 cm (without horns)
71	New Palace, Knossos	AMH	H 34·5 cm
72–73	New Palace, Knossos	AMH	L 19·5 cm
74	New Palace, Knossos	AMH	H of extant part 44 cm
76	New Palace, Knossos	AMH	H of extant part 86 cm
77	New Palace, Knossos	AMH	L 29·5 cm
78	New Palace, Knossos	AMH	L 2·5 to 4 cm; H 3 to 5 cm
79	House of the Frescoes	AMH	H of painted part 60 cm
80	New Palace, Knossos	AMH	H of painted part 25 cm
81	New Palace, Knossos	AMH	H of extant part 37 cm
82	New Palace, Knossos	AMH	H 18·5 cm
83	New Palace, Knossos	AMH	L 1·5 m; B 58 cm
84 a	Mesara	MET	L 2 to 2·5 cm
84 b	Mesara	MET	D 3·5 cm
85	Mesara	MET	L (average) 2 cm
86	Isopata, Knossos	AMH	L 2·6 cm
87	Mavro Spilio, Knossos	AMH	H 3·3 cm
88	New Palace, Knossos	AMH	l H 78 cm
			r H 70 cm
89	New Palace, Knossos	AMH	H 69 cm
95	Katsamba	AMH	H 9·2 cm; D 8·5 cm
96	Katsamba	AMH	H 10·5 cm
97	Amnisos	AMH	H of painted part 1·80 m
98	Phourni, Arkhanes	AMH	l H 5·7 cm; L 1·9 cm; B 1·3 cm
			r four parts each 47 × 47 cm
99 a	Phourni	AMH	L 1·25 m; H 80/98 cm; B 53 cm
104	Tylissos	AMH	H 65 cm
105	Tylissos	AMH	l H 16·5 cm
			r H 25 cm
113	New Palace, Phaistos	AMH	D 16 cm
115	New Palace, Phaistos	AMH	H 29 cm
118	New Palace, Phaistos	AMH	H 16·5 cm
120	Kamilari	AMH	L 16 cm; B 10 cm; H 10 cm
121	Kamilari	AMH	H 14 cm
122	Mesara	MET	H 13 cm; B 16 cm
123	Mesara	MET	smallest 4 × 3 cm; largest 25 × 17 cm
130	Hagia Triada	AMH	H 11·5 cm; D 10 cm
132–133	Hagia Triada	AMH	H of vessel 50 cm
134–136	Hagia Triada	AMH	H of relief 7·5 cm
137–140	Hagia Triada	AMH	L 1·37 m; H of figures 15 cm
145	New Palace, Mallia	Mallia	H of pithos 1·70 cm
148 a	Chrysolakkos, Mallia	AMH	B 4·7 cm
148 b	New Palace, Mallia	AMH	L 14·5 cm
149	New Palace, Mallia	Mallia	D 90 cm
150/151	Old Palace, Mallia	Mallia	H of pithos 2 m
153	Pachyammos, Gournia	AMH	L 1·23 m; H 48 cm
154	Gournia	AMH	L 1·17 m; H 46·5 cm
156	Pseira	AMH	H 28 cm
158	Pseira	AMH	l H 77 cm
			r H 88 cm
159	Pseira	AMH	H 20 cm
161	Palaikastro	AMH	L 1·23 m
162	Sitia	MET	H 16·5 cm; D 19 cm
171 a	Kato Zakro	AMH	D 14 cm
171 b	Kato Zakro	AMH	L 24 cm
172–173	Kato Zakro	AMH	5 × 4·8 cm
174	Kato Zakro	AMH	H 28 cm
176	Kato Zakro	AMH	H 27 cm
178	Kato Zakro	AMH	H 52 cm
180	Kato Zakro	AMH	H 13 cm (without horns)
184	Kato Zakro	AMH	H 24 cm
185	Kato Zakro	AMH	H 33 cm
187	Kato Zakro	AMH	H 16·5 cm (20 cm with handle)
188	Kato Zakro	AMH	D 10·5 cm
189	Kato Zakro	AMH	H 32·5 cm
190	Kato Zakro	AMH	H 38 cm
191	Kato Zakro	AMH	l H 30 cm
			r H 28 cm
192–194	Kato Zakro	AMH	H 37 cm
195 a	Kato Zakro	AMH	H 12·5 cm
196 a	Kato Zakro	AMH	2·5 × 4·5 cm
196 b	Kato Zakro	AMH	7 × 5·5 cm
199	Grivigla	AMH	l H 29 cm
			r H 30 cm
200–201	Mavro Spelio, Knossos	AMH	H 10 cm
202	Palaikastro	AMH	D 18 cm; H 14·3 cm
203	Gournia	AMH	H 15·5 cm
204	Gortyn	AMH	H 52 cm
205	Gazi	AMH	H 79 cm
206	Gazi	AMH	H 58 cm
207	Gazi	AMH	H 52·5 cm
208	Karphi	AMH	H 85 cm
209	Karphi	AMH	H 85 cm
212	Gortyn	AMH	H 34 cm
213	Arkhanes	AMH	H 22 cm
214	Fortetsa, Knossos	AMH	H 12·5 cm
220	Gortyn	AMH	H 1·50 m
221	Gortyn	AMH	H 22 cm
223	Rhezenia	AMH	H 76 cm
224	Idaean Cave	AMH	D 55 cm
227	Arkades	MET	H 20·5 cm
229	Praisos	AMH	L 60 cm

All the photographs in this book
are by Leonard von Matt, Photograph SWB, Buochs, Switzerland,
with the exception of those on
pages 32, 53, 101, 148 (above), by
Professor Max Hirmer, Munich;
that on page 95, from the Heraklion
Museum Archive; those on pages
98, 99 (below), by Mr John Sakellarakis, Deputy Curator of the
Archaeological Museum,
Heraklion.

The plans of the Palaces of Knossos
(ground floor, Piano Nobile),
Phaistos, and Mallia are after Dr
Stylianos Alexiou (*Minoikos Politismos*), by kind permission of the
author; that of the Villa at Hagia
Triada, after J. Bowman (*Crete*);
that of the Palace of Kato Zakro
(stage of excavation reached in
1966), by kind permission of Professor Nikolaos Platon.